Sonship According to The Kingdom

Endorsements

Sadly, many believers never come to a true understanding of who they really are in Christ. Paul rebuked the Corinthians for acting like mere humans. We are more than saved sinners; we are new creations. As sons and daughters of the Most High God, we're filled with His Spirit, infused with His nature, heirs in His kingdom, and partners in His great cause. You *will* come to a greater revelation of this as you read Greg Hood's powerful book *Sonship According to the Kingdom*.

Dr. Dutch Sheets
Dutch Sheets Ministries and *Give Him 15* daily prayer and decrees.
Bestselling author of: *Authority in Prayer, An Appeal to Heaven, Intercessory Prayer*

As I ponder on Jewels in the Lord's Treasury, that at times have been lost and must be rediscovered, I am drawn to three words that start with the Letter "I". These are not just catchy words or phrases, but rather character traits. These are: 1) Integrity... 2) Intensity... and 3) Identity... It would easy for me to add in some of my other favorite Kingdom "I" Words such as "Intercession" and "Intentionally" and others.

But let me tell you a secret. I was having dinner with my new friend, Greg Hood, and I was multi-tasking in the Spirit, as I quietly often am. I saw the Letter "I" written in his eye. As we sat there, I asked the Holy Spirit what this was all about. I heard, "This man has his gaze set on raising up Kingdom Equippers who will have integrity in their inward parts. He does everything with intensity unto the end goal that their identity will be rooted and grounded in the Word of God."

The Gospel of the Kingdom

Thus, I have the honor of endorsing Dr. Greg Hood's book, *Sonship According to the Kingdom*.

Equipped to Be An Equipper!

Dr. James W Goll
God Encounters Ministries, GOLL Ideation LLC

Nations are in a crisis driven largely by the curse of fatherlessness and the breakdown of the nuclear family unit. The solution: reversing the curse through *Sonship According to the Kingdom*. We belong. We are His. We are not forsaken. We are not orphans. He has taken fatherhood responsibility for us. This powerful book, penned by my friend Greg Hood, holds the keys not just for a transformed life but for the power to change the world!

Jane Hamon
Apostle, Vision Church @ Christian International
Author: *Dreams and Visions, The Deborah Company, The Cyrus Decree, Discernment and Declarations for Breakthrough*

Sonship According to the Kingdom takes the reader on a thoughtful journey through what it means to be a child of God. Greg Hood demonstrates a passion to see people live life to the fullest. To do so, he points out, we must understand the resources at our disposal. Gone are the days when Christians can rationalize away a weak faith. *Sonship According to the Kingdom* challenges the reader to see tangible evidence of a life devoted to Christ. Those content with a mediocre lifestyle need not read this book.

Christina Bobb
Attorney for President Donald J. Trump
Author, *Stealing Your Vote: The Inside Story of the 2020 Election and What It Means for 2024*

Endorsements

Functioning in the miraculous power of the Lord, walking through test and trials and/or being used to impact the world with the kingdom of God requires essentially one thing. That thing is a revelation of who we are as the sons of God. When we, by the revelation of the Spirit of God, recognize our status with God, rejection vanishes and empowerment comes. My longtime friend, Greg Hood, does a masterful job of highlighting these truths in his new book *Sonship According to the Kingdom*. You will not be disappointed in your investment of this book. It could change your life!

Robert Henderson
Best-Selling Author of *The Courts of Heaven* series

In the 1500-year-old classic book by Sun Tzu: *The Art of War*, we are reminded that for victory, "one must know their enemy...many fail to see that for victory, one must know themselves...." Dr. Greg Hood has hit the mark in his new book *Sonship According to the Kingdom*. He declares forcefully the importance of Kingdom believers embracing and living out their new identity in Christ. This powerful volume will unleash Kingdom potential in all who grasp its powerful truths....

Dr. Ron Phillips, D. Min
Pastor Emeritus Abba's House, Chattanooga, TN
Fresh Oil Ministries

This book is a must-read! I was informed, enlightened, and impacted as I devoured the pages of this well-written and very understandable volume!

I love the way Greg wove together a tapestry of Biblical, theological, historical, and autobiographical strands to present the revelation of the Kingdom of God, and its expression and ministry, in the earth through the sons and daughters of the Lord God. There are many places in the book where you will laugh as you are learning.

The heart of this book will assist the followers of King Jesus to be prepared for life and ministry as each one sees his or her identity as a son or a daughter of Father God and a member of His family.

This truth comes into clear focus when Greg contrasts religion and relationship. This is a root issue for everyone. According to Scripture, religion produces slaves while relationship develops sons and daughters in the Kingdom. Slaves do not inherit; sons and daughters inherit. They are the ones who share in Christ's inheritance! Also presented in this contrast between religion and relationship is the fact that religion tends to breed condemnation, either of self or of others. On the other hand, relationship breeds liberation among the people of God. The Apostle Paul in Romans 8 reminds us that our liberation (freedom) leads to the liberation and freedom of the created order which, of course, includes nations!

In Matthew 13:38, Christ calls His disciples "sons of the Kingdom." In this verse, Jesus also refers to the 'sons of the Evil one'. Mark it down, the battle for the Earth is between "the sons." Paul refers to the battle as between the sons of light and the sons of darkness. Another instructive contrast in the book is between spiritual adoption and spiritual orphanhood. Every person, though loved, is a spiritual orphan until he or she is adopted by Father God. The spirit of adoption causes our hearts to cry out, "Abba, Daddy God." The bottom line is: it is the covenant family of God, i.e., His sons and daughters, who are the agents of the advancement of God's kingdom in history!

I cannot recommend this life-changing and world-changing book too highly! Use it for your own spiritual growth, and use it as a teaching manual for others! Dr. Greg Hood is among several outstanding Kingdom leaders who are clear voices for truth at this time in history. I am very impressed by him and his ministry gifts. In my understanding, he is an apostolic prophet. Others might see him as a prophetic apostle. In addition, he carries a strong anointing as a gifted teacher in the Body of Christ.

Endorsements

This is a season of the unveiling of the spirit of wisdom and revelation to the Body of Christ. This volume, *Sonship According to the Kingdom*, will be used of God to release these realities to you and many!

Dr. Jim Hodges
Federation of Ministers and Churches International
Cedar Hill, TX

Backed by scriptural truth, Greg Hood, in his new book *Sonship According to the Kingdom*, navigates the reader through the legitimate process of maturing in Christ and being conformed into His Image. He exposes the counterfeit life that is bent on obtaining the approval of man and man-made success through striving. He rightly divides this against living an abundant life in true fellowship with God that will wait on Him to define success, as our souls prosper. Greg's life and ministry demonstrate Romans 8:14... "For all who are being led by the Spirit of God, these are sons of God."

Congressman Josh Bercheen
Oklahoma's Second Congressional District, 118th Congress

I can't tell you how refreshing it is to see someone writing a book on "Sonship." Greg has captured the heart of our Father on a subject that is close to His heart. It is one of my favorite things to study and preach on. To know that our Lord wants to communicate with us as sons and not traditional church people. With the help of this writing, *Sonship According to the Kingdom*, we can shift from an orphanage mentality into a kingdom mentality of SONS. I know this book will transform the heart of many believers. Thanks, Greg, for putting our Father's heart into words.

Apostle Ken Malone
Kingdom Gate Worship Center, Satellite Beach, Florida

In his new book, Dr. Greg Hood said, "In our study of the Kingdom of God, we are putting a knife to the throat of the spirit of religion," and he meant every word! His next salvo aimed at the demonic effects of the spirit of religion is found in his new offering, *Sonship According to the Kingdom—Stepping into the Power of Your True Identity*. For many generations, the Church [as we know it] has suffered an identity crisis of cosmic proportions. The enemy understands that if we [believers] don't know who we are in Christ, we are forever assigned to wander around in the wilderness in a state of discontent and disillusionment, much like the Children of Israel – always in motion but never reaching the Promised Land [of our true identity]. He has exposed this demonic deception with a brilliant exposition of Scripture, keen insight, and many practical applications.

Dr. Hood's thesis is stated in plain language: "Folks, we are not powerless. We are not impoverished spectators reduced to passive waiting. We are children of God, maturing to sons and daughters, taking our part in establishing the Kingdom of God." To which I say, Amen and Amen!

I recommend that you take your time and allow the revelation presented in this book to challenge any sacred cows that might still be lurking around trying to convince you that you are not a son or daughter of the King with royal blood flowing through your veins.

Dr. J. Tod Zeiger, D. Min
President, Tod Zeiger Ministries, Friendsville, Tennessee 37737

Dr. Greg Hood has done it again! This is teaching you can trust and revelation that gets results! In the pages of this book, you will find out what the Lord Jesus is saying and doing, where He is going and how you can walk with Him into the fulness of sonship so that you can be an expression of the kingdom of God here upon the earth. It is through your internal development, becoming a full-grown son of God, that you step into the full manifestation of your external achievement in Jesus! The series of revelations given in this book

Endorsements

provide a pathway into the ability to both experience and share the manifest presence and power of God for others to benefit and enjoy the Lord Jesus! Prepare for transition, transformation, and transfiguration by the glory of God that's about to be imparted to you by the Spirit of the Lord as you read Greg's book!

Apostle Tony Kemp
President of ACTS GROUP
Tony Kemp Ministries

I see a lot of books written about the needs of modern Christianity. It seems that every person with a word processor and a Bible has a ready-made answer to the perceived problems facing the church today. But no one zeroes in on the key issue the way Greg Hood does in *Sonship According to the Kingdom*.

We don't need more preaching. We don't need stricter hierarchy. We don't need more seminaries or cathedrals. We need to face ourselves squarely and honestly, standing before Almighty God, and confront what we are: the good, the bad, and the ugly.

We are the Church, the Body of Christ, but do we know what that means? Are we sons and daughters of the Kingdom of God? Or are we simply children mired in religion, that conglomeration of rituals, observances, hierarchy and tradition? Are we destined to remain what we've always been? Or are we ready to step into the next level that God has revealed to us—that which has always existed?

As Greg points out, religion flourishes where God's reality is obscured by darkness. Said another way, religion is what you get when you lack the vital, living connection with the Spirit of God. At best, religion is a placeholder until that which is perfect comes. At worst, religion is the poison we feed our children, saying "eat it, it's good for you," as we go about our lives of quiet desperation.

As Greg says, religion is not evil; it is merely incomplete. Half a wheel on my car doesn't bother me as long as it's sitting in the driveway. But when it's time to hit the road, I need something that works.

The church today needs a complete theology. We are not mere children. We are not bondservants. We are maturing sons and daughters of God rising up to grasp the destiny before us. Funny how destiny looks a lot like work. So be it. The Kingdom of God is not an obligation. It is a privilege. Man was not placed in the garden to lounge around. He had a job; a purpose.

It's time to work, embracing in a new paradigm. We are not prodigals slaving away in foreign pigsties. We are coming home to Father's estate. Yes, we are greeted with a robe and a ring and sandals, but the day after—the part that the parable leaves off—is when we're handed a sickle and sent to join the harvest.

Sons and daughters embrace their purpose in the kingdom, and they receive the reward of their labors as joint heirs with Christ.

Dr. Harold Eberle, Worldcast Ministries, Yakima WA
Author of numerous books including *Father Son Theology*.

If you want to understand who you are in Christ and want to break both religious and cultural views on being a son of God. Do we have a book for you! If you want to know how much authority a son of God walks in. Do we have a book for you! Greg, in this book, does not just give you revelation of Sonship but helps you grasp in a very eye-opening way, why you have not been able to walk into your true identity; His way of leading you into truth is inspiring and awakening to say the least. Well written and worth reading and sharing with others. We live in a generation that needs to find its true identity and then, "turn our world upside down once again."

I strongly recommend this book for all who want to walk in the fullness of their potential.

Apostle Dennis Goldsworthy-Davis
Open Wells Ministry, San Antonio, TX

Endorsements

Dr. Greg Hood has stepped into a new season of leadership fathering. His kingdom assignment reaches beyond a local church experience and embraces a new nation of believers. As I read this book, my heart was settled, encouraged, and challenged. The anticipation of sonship being released is found in the practical way that this author embraces the truth and reality of the kingdom and brings it into everyday experiences. This book is real, at times raw, and in a deep sense elevates the reader to a new place of walking in a level of understanding and authority that was evident in the early church.

The people of God will not accelerate without a biblical and accurate understanding of the true operation of the Kingdom of God on the earth. We cannot afford to simply replace words like "Church," with "Ekklesia," and continuing doing life as we have always done it. The Ekklesia must have a foundation upon which to advance. Therein, you find Dr. Hood's passion and calling. It comes to the forefront in this deeply authentic book, *Sonship According to the Kingdom*. This is not just a book for five-fold leaders, this is a book for every person who is "called out of darkness, and into the light!"

Dr. Scott Reece
River City Church, Quad Cities

One of the major strongholds in modern Christianity is an orphan spirit. I am convinced that the orphan spirit is caused by a lack of true identity. True identity comes not just from having a Father, but from understanding that your Father is a King and that you are a child of the King. Dr. Hood has done an amazing job of revealing to us our true identity as sons and not slaves. In his work on *Sonship According to the Kingdom*, he not only helps us understand our true identity, but also returns us to the Father's original intent for our lives, thus restoring our Kingdom Purpose!

Dr. Hood's book *Sonship According to the Kingdom* is a must-read for all those searching for their Kingdom Identity and Purpose.

Dr. Dwain Miller, Ph.D.
Senior Pastor, The Edge Church, Cabot, AR

The timeliness of Dr. Greg Hood's book is impeccable timing. In a world that has lost its identity and biblical mooring, this book is on time and on target. *Sonship According to the Kingdom* challenges our norms that tend to only give us hindsight but no foresight. You will be able to understand the difference between truth and revelation and to be able to (2 Peter 1:12) apply present truth. This book will help you understand why truth plus additions have created traditions that have stifled the church. Greg masterfully reveals the pathway for maturity from being a child to becoming Sons of the Kingdom where the true inheritance can be received. Anyone reading this book will have broken off any lingering dust of an orphan spirit which blinds us from seeing our redemptive identity. You will clearly get to see the benefits of entering the culture of the Kingdom of God shaking loose from the cultures of this world. Buy it! Read it! Share it!

Kerry Kirkwood, Senior Pastor
Trinity Fellowship Church, Tyler, Texas

God is raising up spiritual sons, who will align their hearts perfectly with God's purposes for this new season. Many candidates lack understanding of their identity or may not even be aware of it. Even if they understand the concept, the question remains, "Is it a "working" identity? Moving and functioning beyond just theory, active and maturing as God intends?"

In this new book by Greg Hood, *Sonship According to the Kingdom*, Greg Hood gives much needed clarification as to what God is doing and expects of us as "sons." Please allow me to recommend

Endorsements

this excellent resource to those seeking Kingdom union and fullness in God.

Accomplishing anything great for the Kingdom requires significant understanding of the role and assignment you have. At times we encounter seemingly insurmountable obstacles, hardships, "holy disruptions," and we may not feel like a "son." Immaturity or wrong choices can cause you to drift out of the lane God has prepared for you. Bumps at the edge of the road, are meant to awaken you to change your way of thinking.

Feelings don't change your standing in God. To fulfill your assignment, you must change! It's time. Things can't stay the way they've been. You just need an identity shift. In this now and necessary message, Greg's teaching, makes your position in God clear and invites you to be empowered, even while you are in process.

Trust the process!!

Pastor Jerry Bryant,
Worship City Alliance, Nashville, TN
www.worshipcityalliance.com

Wow, here he goes again. Somewhat quoting from scripture, "can anything good come from a redneck Mississippian?" The answer to that one is simple, "yes." I have been in church leadership, primarily as a pastor, for forty-five years. I've often told people that the most asked question that I have ever received from those that I serve has been, "what is God's call for my life?" In my early years I would try desperately to help counsel them through the many decisions that affected their upcoming occupations or their roles in society. I often wished that I had a little black book in my pocket that I could use to help people with their decision. As a matter of fact, I often wondered if my name was in that little black book as I sometimes even questioned my own call. Several years ago, as I asked the Lord about this, He gave me a rather profound and peculiar response. He said, "I could care less what occupation a person has." What? As I continued to seek out what this meant He then began to release this same revelation that Greg is now sharing about in this book. Our call is to be a son and daughter of the Most High God. Our call is to be a king and a priest in His Kingdom. We might be a dishwasher in a restaurant. We might be a legislator in the halls of government. We might be a teacher or a housewife. We might be a plumber, or we might be a surgeon. We might be a musician in a rock band or an actor on the big screen. But whatever our occupation – our call is to be a son or a daughter of God through our brother and co-heir Christ Jesus. As you read *Sonship According to the Kingdom* your mindset will be profoundly transformed. For so many decades our identity, especially with the church, was limited only to sitting in the pew or carrying out the duties of church programs in a religious structure. Get ready! That is not your destiny. We are to be transformers, reformers and sons and daughters who will manifest the very will and kingdom of our Father. You will probably be offended by many things that you read in this book, but through it all, you will discover who you are!

Dr. Tom Schlueter, Apostle
Texas Apostolic Prayer Network
Prince of Peace House of Prayer, Arlington, Texas

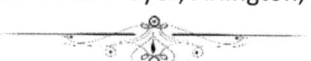

Dr. Greg Hood has written an excellent work in *Sonship According to the Kingdom*. This book calls for each believer to embrace and grow into the fullness of their identity in Christ. Most Christian's live way below their potential and rarely fulfill their destiny in God's Kingdom. This is because they lack an accurate and complete revelation of their sonship. Scripture teaches that we are deeply loved by our Father and have been adopted into His family. Therefore, we are not to live as slaves, but as sons who are privileged to have unrestricted access to our Father and to all that is His (John 15:15).

I believe that we are living in a time when the LORD is releasing a clear and complete revelation of His goodness. We must have ears to hear! Hosea saw a last days move of God that would result in a people

Endorsements

who would "return and seek the Lord their God and David their king; and they will come trembling to the Lord and to His goodness in the last days" (Hosea 3:5, NASB). In *Sonship According to the Kingdom*, Greg Hood masterfully weaves together Scripture and stories to challenge us to live and love as sons. It is obvious that Greg speaks out of the depths of the wellspring of one who has known the Father in a deeply intimate manner for quite some time.

Glenn Bleakney
Awake Nations Ministries
The Kingdom Community

One of the assignments of those whom God has positioned as a five-fold ministry gift is to bring people to a revelation of who they truly are in Christ, thus provoking them to take and embrace the journey that advances their spiritual growth. Spiritual growth produces mature sons who are equipped and able to take their place in the advancement of the Kingdom of God. In his book, *Sonship According to the Kingdom*, my friend, Greg Hood exemplifies that assignment. As you read these pages, you will be challenged to go deeper in your understanding of sonship and Kingdom, and you will be greatly inspired by the uncovering of these scriptural revelations.

Gina Gholston
Author, *Awakening the Church to Awaken a Nation* and *Dreams of Awakening*

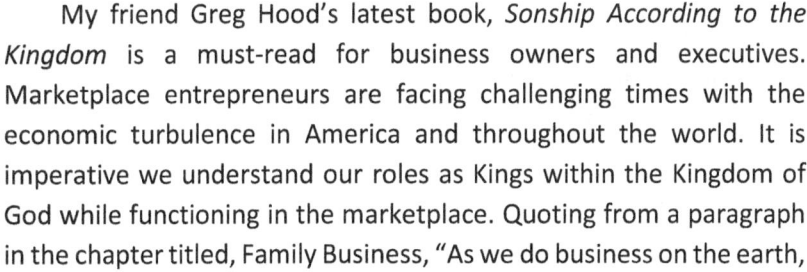

My friend Greg Hood's latest book, *Sonship According to the Kingdom* is a must-read for business owners and executives. Marketplace entrepreneurs are facing challenging times with the economic turbulence in America and throughout the world. It is imperative we understand our roles as Kings within the Kingdom of God while functioning in the marketplace. Quoting from a paragraph in the chapter titled, Family Business, "As we do business on the earth, we will do different things in the kingdom, but we are kings doing those things. We are not on earth to make a living. We are here to bring life to all we do. We need to see ourselves as kings". The marketplace desperately needs to be saturated with business owners who clearly understand kingdom and how it effects the health of their businesses and the economy. This book is filled with priceless concepts throughout each chapter. I highly recommend *Sonship According to the Kingdom* to everyone that functions in the marketplace.

Terry M. Wise
Serial Entrepreneur, Co-Founder Genesis A New Beginning and TMS of the Carolinas

In the 1960s, there was a TV commercial from the brokerage firm E.F. Hutton. The closing words of the commercial were "when E.F. Hutton speaks, people listen." Greg Hood is a modern E.F. Hutton prophetic voice. When he speaks, people listen. His new book, *Sonship According to the Kingdom—Stepping into the Power of Your True Identity,* is a much-needed word the modern-day church must hear and apply to advance the Kingdom. For too long the church has faltered by what it means to be sons and daughters of the King of Kings. With the wit and humor of a "Mississippi boy," he delivers this message in simple yet profound clarity. His goal is not to just give us more information but to bring transformation. As you read and "hear" this message, be ready to be brought to a new dimension of identity and Kingdom living.

David Black
Gold Monarch Healing Center
Abilene, Texas

Endorsements

I was excited when asked by my friend Greg Hood to read and write an endorsement for his next book *Sonship According to the Kingdom*.

Greg writes in a manner that comes from his strength of Kingdom understanding and the sonship he walks in every day of his life. He paints a wide-stroke picture of sonship lifestyle. To operate as a son of God, we must destroy the false alter of belief systems and learned behaviors that the religious desire their followers to camp around. Greg clearly communicates that sonship is relational and not just a learned behavior. The religious say that God's word says, "obey my commandments if you love me." God's word actually says, "if, or as you love me, keep my commands." Love functions deeply relationally. Commandments without love are simply learned behaviors. In my endorsement of Greg's writings, I not only encourage you in the reading of this book, I challenge you to purchase more copies and sow it into people's lives you care about. Their reading of this book will benefit their life, to be positioned for God to restore the foundation of sonship in and through them. Yes, words upon these pages carry the potential and purpose to set a captive free, to lead them into the captivity of authentic life-giving sonship.

Clay Nash
Claynash.org
Author of *Activating the Prophetic, Relational Authority, God Dreams to Make America Great Again*, and contributor to *The Real Deal* by Jim Bryson.

I've heard it said that when we are young, life is about learning how to grow, but when we received our assignment from God, Life becomes about growing others. And that is exactly what Dr. Greg Hood has done in his book *Sonship According to the Kingdom*.

Dr. Hood is an influential voice in God's Kingdom. His sermons, books, conferences and Kingdom University have ignited the hearts and minds of people to understand the Bible and our true identity in Christ. This book extends his understanding of the Sonship of the Kingdom by giving the reader insightful, informative and challenging content to motivate us all to live a life of freedom from the modern-day religion and live a life of purpose, power and faith.

Coach Scott Oatsvall
Health Coach, LT360Health.com

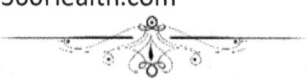

Greg's new book *Sonship According to the Kingdom* will make you laugh one minute while the next minute you will be immersed in deep Biblical Truth that is sorely needed these days! Greg exposes "Religion" for what it is while at the same time he brings life-giving revelation that will change your life. You will fall more in love with the Bible than ever before. *Sonship According to the Kingdom* brings clear and plain understanding of the fullness of who Jesus IS and who you ARE. Don't miss this book!

Bob Long, Rally Call Ministries

Greg Hood is "a man after God's own Heart" Everywhere he ministers around the World he carries the Father's heart. What is so greatly needed today is understanding and revelation of what it means to be sons, not orphans. In his book, *Sonship According to the Kingdom*, we find key understandings and simple revelation on true identity. I can't speak enough on it. This book will change your life!

Evangelist Mike Barrett
Transformation Ministries, Gold Coast, Australia

Dr. Hood offers a treasure trove of deep insight and revelation on the critical area of understanding "sonship". This book is so well written. It is full of real-life stories, real-life applicable truths, and perhaps most important, real-life marketplace applications. If you

Endorsements

want to understand how to navigate through a spiritual minefield, then *Sonship According to the Kingdom* is your go to training manual to accompany your Bible.

David Dalton, Founder, eBars, Franklin, TN, www.ebars.com

My family and I have gotten to LOVE Dr. Greg Hood and his beautiful wife Joan! We have known them for several years now since we first met them in Hawaii. It was "love at first sight" when we met at a backyard gathering at our home! They are truly an amazing couple, with great hearts, who loves God and loves teaching the true word of God! Dr. Greg's wisdom and understanding of the scripture is unbelievable! He is definitely gifted to teach the word, keeping it simple for all to understand. I love the clarity on how he breaks things down to simple and easy to understand steps that can be applied in our day-to-day lives, including family and business! I am certainly not an expert on the Bible, but my understanding from Dr. Greg's teaching has helped to build my personal relationship with the Father and my walk with him in his Kingdom. Many people are confused with religion and don't understand relationship, and there's no better person than Dr. Greg Hood to teach you this truth! I am grateful to Dr. Greg Hood and his wife Joan for enriching my life and my families lives with his wisdom and teaching! This book is another blessing in my life, and I encourage all of you to read it.

Irene Brackenridge
Business Owner
Senior Vice President, Primerica Financial Services

What an honor it is to endorse this newest book by Apostle Greg Hood, *Sonship According to the Kingdom*. The Western mindset of sonship has truly limited our understanding of this valuable Kingdom role. Apostle Greg's light-hearted, joyful ability to take these concepts and integrate them into our lifestyle is spectacular. He causes the reader to desire to delve further and further into the pages and receive the Father's love and passion for our identity to be revealed. It is important to know that zeal for our destiny and for the Lord enables us to endure the qualification process into transformation from being a child of God into a son of God. Enjoy your process in the Kingdom!

>**Rodney Orsborn**, Apostolic Leader, Master's Arrow Ministries
>The Epicenter in Amarillo Texas
>Author of *The Mantle and Anointing of Stephen* and *House 2 House Workbook*.

What an amazing and ground-breaking book! Dr. Greg Hood's book "Sonship according to the Kingdom" is packed with fresh revelation and insight for where the church is at today, and will impact generations to come. Greg has given us a rich understanding in the scriptures of the Spirit of Adoption, the very heart of the Gospel, and exposes the religious traditions that have held the church in bondage. This book will recalibrate your life! It will connect you with God's original intent and plan, and you will be drawing from the deep truths and rich treasures for many years. I know I will! I especially recommend this book to all who are interested in hearing what the Spirit is saying to the church in this hour. Thank you, Dr. Greg!

>**Prophet Faylene Sparks**
>Australia Company of Seers

Sonship According to The Kingdom

Stepping Into the Power Of Your True Identity

Greg Hood

Copyright

Sonship According to the Kingdom

by Greg Hood

Copyright © 2023 by Greg Hood (Greg Hood Ministries)

All rights reserved. This book is protected by the copyright laws of the United States of America. This book may not be copied or reprinted for commercial gain or profit. The use of short quotations or occasional page copying for personal or group study is encouraged. Permission will be granted upon request from Greg Hood. All rights reserved. Any emphasis added to scripture quotations is the author's own.

Unless otherwise noted, scripture quotations are taken from the New American Standard Bible, © 1960, 1962, 1963, 1968, 1971, 1972, 1973, 1975, 1977, 1995 by the Lockman Foundation.

Word studies in the Greek and Hebrew are taken from:

- Strong's Concordance
- Brown-Driver-Briggs Hebrew and English Lexicon
- Theological Dictionary of the New Testament © 1985 William B. Eerdmans Publishing Company
- AMG's Annotated Dictionary of the Old and New Testament ©1984, 1990, 2008
- The Complete Word Study Dictionary: Old Testament by Warren Baker and Eugene Carpenter ©2003
- The Complete Word Study Dictionary: New Testament compiled by Spiros Zodhiates ©1992
- Expositor's Greek New Testament, Volumes 1-5: George H. Doran Company ©1897 New York

Edit/Layout by Jim Bryson (JamesLBryson@gmail.com)

Cover design by David Munoz (davidmunoznvtn@gmail.com)

Contact Info

    Dr. Greg Hood, Th.D.
    Greg Hood Ministries
    1113 Murfreesboro Rd
    Suite 106 #222
    Franklin TN 37064
    United States
    office@greghood.org

Contents

Foreword .... - 1 -

Preface .... - 7 -

1. Understanding Scripture .... - 15 -

2. Identity Shift .... - 19 -

3. Family Business .... - 45 -

4. Dominion of the King .... - 77 -

5. Reestablishing Identity .... - 105 -

6. Mindset Matters .... - 131 -

7. Child to Son .... - 159 -

8. Conclusion .... - 179 -

Appendix .... - 183 -

About the Author .... - 193 -

Previous Work .... - 195 -

Kingdom University .... - 203 -

Dedication

I DEDICATE THIS BOOK to my Pawpaw Joe (Joseph Wilber Oliver), who greatly influenced my life and my calling to ministry. A man who served in ministry for 75 years, he was a church planter and a missionary. He planted a Bible school and oversaw churches and ministers in all the places he served. He set the bar for what a man should be. I pray I will achieve that high mark before I leave this earth. I love you, Pawpaw, and I am thankful for your influence, correction and love toward me as your grandson.

Acknowledgments

I WANT TO THANK MY WIFE, JOAN, who has listened to me countless times teaching on the topic of sonship. She has watched and participated in the reshaping of my school of thought as it progressed from a staunch religious mindset to a kingdom mindset. She is my rock and the love of my life.

I want to thank my eldest son, Micah Dean Hood, for being the very handsome cover model on the front of this book. (Man, he looks a lot like his dad! LOL!) Thank you, Son, for your willingness to do this. I love you beyond words. I know you will step into the power of your true identity in a much greater way in the days, months and years that are ahead of you.

Thank you to my mother, Ann Hood, who took the photo of my grandfather's (her father's) old barn that we have placed on the back cover of this book. Thank you for leading me to the Lord when I was eight years old. Your unconditional love set me on this journey, and your godly example has helped me stay the course.

A very special thanks to my editor, Jim Bryson. You are not only a great editor, but you have become a wonderful friend. I am thankful. You have worked through this manuscript at the speed of light, and like an arrow shot from a master bowman's bow, you have hit the mark.

To my friend Tim Sheets, who wrote the Foreword, and to all my friends who gave endorsements for this book (and who did not require payment, lol!), thank you!

To those who gave me theological insight (and correction from time to time) for this work, I am eternally grateful. You all have impacted my life in very special ways. I am thankful for our friendships.

A special thank you to Pastor Terry Garrett and Carrol McDonnell for assisting in proofreading.

Foreword

by Tim Sheets

THE SUBJECT OF SONSHIP that Apostle Greg Hood has chosen for this book, Sonship of the Kingdom, is vital for our times. Its biblical understanding is indeed life-changing. Sadly, because of nominal religion's portrayal of Father God, much of our world has the wrong perspective of who God really is. Those wrong perspectives hinder our receiving of greater revelation about the nature of God. They filter what we can and cannot accept. God can present himself to us fifty different ways, but until our concept of God is open to those new ways, we will remain ignorant of the ever-expanding nature of God.

Sonship According to the Kingdom is the enlightenment we need to further our understanding, indeed, our relationship, with Father God. So many live in fear of our great God, not realizing his loving, tender, and gracious nature toward his children. He is not out to get us if we mess up. Let's face it: if he was the vengeful, unforgiving God as portrayed by religion, we'd all be dead by now. Fortunately, his desire is to lovingly mentor us, shaping our lives into plans and purposes that bring out the best in us—the best as we were created to be.

Religion says:

"I messed up. Dad is going to kill me!"

Sonship says:

"I messed up. I need to call Dad."

Sonship According to the Kingdom

The distinction is fear vs. trust, punishment vs. affection.

The Genesis account of creation describes clearly the intimacy of relationship that Father God desires with us. We see this as God spoke the universe into being. From Genesis 1 and 2, we read:

In the beginning God created the heavens and the earth.

There was a problem with the earth, however.

The earth was a formless and desolate emptiness, and darkness was over the surface of the deep...

Formless...desolate...empty...dark. Ah, the plot thickens. Yet help is on the way.

The Spirit of God was hovering over the surface of the waters.

God's Spirit showed up. Now things get interesting.

Then God said, "Let there be..."

Yes! Anytime you read "God said...," you know great things are about to happen.

Soon, it was time to create mankind.

Then God said, "Let Us make mankind in Our image, according to Our likeness;

And from God's original commission, we understand mankind's purpose.

Be fruitful and multiply, and fill the earth, and subdue it; and rule over the fish of the sea and over the birds of the sky and over every living thing that moves on the earth.

Quite the tall order.

Notice how God created man, however.

Then the Lord God formed the man of dust from the ground, and breathed into his nostrils the breath of life; and the man became a living person.

God formed mankind with his hands the way one might craft a chosen vessel. While most other things in creation were brought forth

Foreword

with God's decree, man was formed by hand as something near and dear to the Creator's heart. Clearly, God wanted his fathering touch to be upon his children. He wanted to be our hands-on Father, engaged in the lives of his sons and daughters—steadying them, holding them, guiding and forgiving them, redeeming and restoring them. From the beginning of creation, God's loving nature was revealed throughout the universe. It's as if God was thinking: *I will relate to man differently than the rest of creation. I will be an involved Father. They will be a part us...in time.*

God had intended more for man than simply lying around the garden and enjoying the cool breeze. Everything that was created prior to mankind was in preparation for our learning, our use and our growth. Implicit in God's commission to the first people was a call to action, to take on tasks that they were not quite ready for. Yes, the equipping was there, but the maturity was not. At least...not yet. Mankind needed to grow up. It is a task that remains to this present day.

When Jesus came to restore the government of God upon the earth, he brought with him a mandate from the Father: *prepare mankind to receive my Spirit in fullness within their hearts.* For it was Holy Spirit who would teach us all things.

Paul understood this when explaining to the Galatians that the Father raises us as children with no rights other than that of a bondservant. This is why God sends teachers, trainers and tutors to raise us into adulthood. God desires fully formed sons and daughters. Children are delightful, but their potential is realized in adulthood. We come into this divine salvation as children, but we walk as mature ones who are trusted and assigned metrons of responsibility. Thus, we fulfill our calling through growth. God nurtures us, cultivates us, challenges us, cajoles us, even cleanses us. We, in turn, stand before him in awe and reverence, becoming like him.

Understanding this fathering nature of God has truly changed my life, and it will do the same for all of us. Paul identifies the born-again ones as heirs. Romans 8:17 tells us we are heirs of God and joint heirs with Christ. As God's children, we are family. What magnificent worth that portrays! We are not merely the stepkids, the ne'er-do-wells or the runts of the litter. We are part of God's family—in name, in deed and in obligation. We walk as maturing sons and daughters, and we accept our callings as such.

The Apostle Paul highlights the tender nature of Father's heart toward his kids in 2 Timothy 1:8-9, where he tells of...

the power of God, who saved us and called us with a holy calling, not according to our works, but according to His own purpose and grace, which was granted to us in Christ Jesus from all eternity...

God has saved us and called us according to his own purpose and grace. The word purpose in the original Greek text is *prothesis*. Pro means "before" and thesis refers to "a written report." Perhaps in high school or college, you had to write a thesis. It is with this understanding that Paul explains our relationship with our heavenly Father. Before you were born, God wrote your thesis. This means your life has spent time in God's mind. He has thought about you—who you would be and what you would do. Further, he has plans for you—good plans! He put those plans in you and gave you what you would need to accomplish them with his help. You are so special to the Father! His desire is to walk with you, assisting your purpose in all the stages of life. From Psalm 139:16:

Your eyes have seen my formless substance;
And in Your book were written
All the days that were ordained for me,
When as yet there was not one of them.

And should we happen to mess up here and there—yeah, we will mess up—we must learn to run to the Father, not away from him. His embrace heals us; his hands steer us; and his heart unfolds our destiny.

Foreword

Apostle Greg explains this amazing revelation of Papa God in great detail. The principles taught in *Sonship According to the Kingdom* will encourage you to walk in a deeper relationship with the Father. They will inspire you to live your life with a sense of confidence and worth. They will provide a healthy understanding of Father's correction. They will align you with Father's family. They will teach you how to be an heir of God and most importantly, they will imbed in you the absolute joy of being his son or daughter.

Apostle Tim Sheets
Author of *Angel Armies, Angel Armies on Assignment, Planting the Heavens*
Tim Sheets Ministries
The Oasis Church, Middletown, Ohio
www.timsheets.org

Preface

by Alemu Beeftu. Ph.D.

AN ID CARD IS VERY IMPORTANT to go anywhere and to do anything. The personal identification card comes in many forms such as a driver's license, passport, etc. All these are to verify if we are who we say we are, and they are external. The Kingdom of God also requires ID which is internal. It is called identity. Individual identity was established by God before the foundation of the earth. It was made known at conception when God named us for His glory and revealed His eternal plan. Isaiah put it this way, "Listen to me, you islands; hear this, you distant nations: Before I was born the Lord called me; from my birth he has made mention of my name." (Is 49:1) Such naming by God is enlightening a true identity for divine purpose and life assignment, as we read it in the calling of Jeremiah, "The word of the Lord came to me, saying, "Before I formed you in the womb I knew you, before you were born, I set you apart; I appointed you as a prophet to the nations." (Jer.1:5). The Lord made a similar assertion about Apostle Paul as well. (Gal. 1). That means our identity begins with God and being revealed by knowing, believing & trusting Him since our identity is in Him.

Hence, faith is the foundation of discovering our identity as sons and daughters of God since our true identity is not external but is an inner quality. Such inner quality is being publicized when we are born again and receive authority to become His children (John1:12). Therefore, we discover our identity by trusting in God and knowing who He is to know who we are in Him, which is the core Godly identity. As such, our call is not to find out or discover our identity, but discovering who we are in a holy, powerful, gracious, forgiving and loving God. That opens the door for us to know who we are in Him and who we ought to be because of Him.

That shifts our values, establishes our identity, and defines our purpose as His children. In this context, value is a result of what we believe about God and about what He said about us. That is why faith is the foundation to walk in kingdom authority as His children which is our true identity and calling. Therefore, faith defines our values such as what we believe and why we believe. Our belief defines our identity by enabling us to answer questions regarding the fundamental questions of life: Who am I? Where Am I? Answering these basic questions gives us a solid foundation in the word of God to understand our purpose in life. We affirm our purpose in the kingdom for a greater impact by defining our mission and by responding to the questions of life such as: Whose am I? What is my assignment on this earth? Once we sincerely say to ourselves, I am in Christ, Christ is in me, I am for Christ and Christ is for me, our identity is not only established, but sealed forever to move from activity to live for the cause of Christ with value, identity, and purpose by saying like Paul – "For to me, to live is Christ and to die is gain".

The kingdom of God is being advanced by individuals with value, identity and purpose (VIP generation). Hence, by faith we become His children, by choice we abide in Him to walking in our identity and by commitment we live for Him to fulfill His purpose.

Dr. Greg Hood has laid out beautifully from the word of God the process of understanding our identity as children of God to advance His kingdom with power and authority. This book, *Sonship According to the Kingdom*, is your GPS for the kingdom journey to know what you believe, who you are and what you are created, saved, and anointed for. Read and study this book to affirm your new identity by abiding in Christ, living for Christ and fulfilling your prophetic destiny

Preface

to glorify the King of Glory by completing your life assignment in His kingdom! Be a part of the VIP generation!

Alemu Beeftu. Ph.D.

Founder, President of Gospel of Glory and Emerging Glory Center

Introduction

I WAS RAISED IN A DEDICATED RELIGIOUS FAMILY. The patriarch of our family was my grandfather, a man of towering stature who allowed me to go with him nearly everywhere he went. He took me to churches where he preached, to cattle auctions where he purchased livestock for the farm, to tractor dealerships, to amazing tent meetings, and even to places where he was pioneering new churches. I grew up in his shadow. And I grew up in the shadow of his mainline denominational church, one that is established throughout the Southern United States.

I don't know if I would have been as enamored with church as I was while growing up if it were not for the affection of my grandfather. I didn't know what God looked like, but I was fairly certain he dressed like a country gentleman and occasionally donned white mule work gloves around the farm. And if God spoke with a deep Southern drawl, I didn't notice.

When I was 17, a profound transition occurred in my life. I experienced the baptism of the Holy Spirit. Suddenly, I knew my life's calling, one that would lead me from the fading footsteps of my family and their denominational church. I was launched into the unknown, entering the frontier to which God was leading me. I knew I would have to let go of the past to embrace the present and receive my destiny.

What attracted me to the revelation of God's Holy Spirit was the light that was now burning in my soul. Places I didn't know were dark were now illuminated, and what they uncovered both thrilled me and disturbed me. I had a lot to learn, and a lot to unlearn...starting with everything that was holding me back.

For centuries, Christians have attempted to please God, thereby ensuring their positions as firmly ensconced in God's hierarchy. The stakes, as preached by fiery preachers such as Jonathan Edwards, were both terrifying and unyielding. It was heaven or hell, and whether the early church leaders of bygone eras truly believed that or not, it's clear that their followers believed it, and that was sufficient to sway the masses. Suffice to say that people were highly motivated to adhere to the words of God as conveyed through the men in power.

Still, not everyone's motives were corrupt. Many people sought God sincerely out of a heart of pure allegiance. As with all of us, they did so with the resources at hand. They did the best they could.

So, when people read Jesus' words, that he would build his church, they erected brush arbors, church buildings, temples and cathedrals. They emptied municipal treasuries for the finest stone masonry, stained glass and pipe organs. They built spires reaching to the heavens and filled their structures with ornate receivers for the devout.

When they read that believers were a royal priesthood, they appointed priests, decked them in royal robes and equipped them with censors and ornate staffs. They gave them elaborate titles, a mystical language (Latin), and towering pulpits to preach to the huddle masses below.

When they read that they should search the scriptures to find eternal life, they commissioned universities worldwide, dedicating themselves to the study and preservation of ancient scriptures. They bestowed lofty degrees on the scholars while mystifying the commoners who could barely read. Scribes, lawyers and doctors filled the cathedrals with the revelations of the learned.

When they read that Christians are to be holy and apart from the world, they built cloistered communities far from the corrupting influences of society. Neophytes, hungry for godliness and identity,

Introduction

made the arduous journey to these refuges, pledging themselves through life-altering vows. Penitent pilgrims visited in awe and took away the aura of reverence entombed there, (not to mention some of the best wine and spirits ever conceived during the Middle Ages).

When they read that the early believers were filled with the Spirit, they took measures to fill their buildings with spirited worship. They chanted in reverence, they sang with frivolity, they danced and spun and cried out to the heavens. They played instruments and beat on timbrels, and in our modern age, filled their stages with amplifiers and microphones that deafened neighboring counties.

When they read that we were to go forth to all nations and teach them, they enacted crusades and evangelistic outreaches. They entreated unbelievers as the lost, striving to usher them into the prescribed ritual of observances that passed for the workings of God's holy church.

In short, they created religion. And in so doing, they gradually killed any chance of knowing the truth behind Jesus' revelation: "The words that I have spoken to you are spirit, and are life" (John 6:33). For centuries, people lived under the dictates of religious dogma. They paid their penance and honored doctrinal purity. They obeyed the laws and decrees of church leaders, and they prayed fervently for a rich reward for all their sacrifice and suffering. They were good people doing the best they could with what they had.

I grew up in one such household. I was loved and cared for. My parents and grandparents were good, moral people. They loved me and fed me, corrected me and encouraged me, and raised me the best they could with what they had. When I received the outpouring of the Holy Spirit and began to learn what it meant to walk in the spirit, I saw what my family lacked, not out of evil intent, but out of ignorance. They simply didn't know, and had they possessed the courage to voice the longing and hunger that arise from serving a system of artifice, one that purports to be the real spiritual reality of God, I'm not sure they would have known where to turn next. Nobody lets go of the functional present without the promise of a better tomorrow. For them, they saw no better future.

Religion is what you get when you don't know any better; when you need answers that make sense; when all you have are sticks, and you are trying to build a mansion. Religion serves a need in people. Much like the animals sacrificed in the Old Testament, it fills a gap for the time being.

For religion as an organization to survive, however, it must draw strength from somewhere, so it draws its energy from the people—their devotion, blind allegiance, selfless toil and finances. Religion is organic in that it arises from people's needs, but it is artificial in that it can only sustain itself through the belief of the people who buy into the system. It is this dysfunctional nature of religion that saps people dry, all the while claiming to be the source of life.

In my early years of ministry, I tried to serve religion, rather, I tried to serve people through religion. And it wasn't long until I understood that it just didn't work. But it's hard to let go of a system that purports to be your answer when there is no better alternative.

Enter the Kingdom of God.

As I began to discover the heart and mind of God, through the words of Jesus and the epistles, I realized how far we had been led astray, and worse—how our religious belief structures held us back from encountering the truth of God. I had found a true relationship with God through Holy Spirit, one that he had been offering throughout the ages.

I want to free people from religion and usher them into the Kingdom of God. This is not a narrow passageway that only the few and faithful (and skinny) can navigate. No, this is a barnyard with the gate thrown wide open while the harpies shriek from the sidelines, "Don't you dare step out of the pig pen!"

I'm here to tell you, my friends, that beyond the pig sty and rusty gate lie pastures of God's verdant love. I want to take you there. I want to share openly and clearly, and let you decide. I want you to realize sonship according to the kingdom.

1

Understanding Scripture

IN WALKING OUT THE KINGDOM OF GOD, we have to ask ourselves some questions to help us understand what we read in the Bible. Here are four important questions to consider when examining scripture.

1. WHO IS SPEAKING?

When we study the Word of God, we need to understand the perspective of the writer and, more importantly, the perspective of the speaker being recorded.

Now, I am not talking about God; he is always talking. Holy Spirit breathes the Word of God. We understand that. But in studying scripture, we must ask: Was Holy Spirit speaking when the passage was recorded? Just because something is in the Bible does not make it truth. Sometimes the Bible records barbaric or despicable acts to make a point. The Bible is unflinchingly honest. That does not mean we follow every example we find there. For example, David committed adultery with Bathsheba and murdered her husband to cover up the resultant pregnancy. Is that an example we are to follow? Of course not. Certainly, God had a reason for recording this, but it was clearly not for us to follow. We are to filter; we are to interpret; we are to think; we are to seek Holy Spirit for understanding. Let us be wise, mature and open to God's wonderful Spirit who teaches us all things. Let us have simple hearts and ready ears to receive it.

2. Who Are They Speaking To?

Asking who the speakers were talking to enables us to discern the culture for which the message or word was being applied. There are idioms that were used in those cultures that don't make sense today. In fact, they mean something totally different to us in modern culture.

We see this everywhere. Expressions in America don't make sense in England. Even expressions in Indiana don't make sense in Mississippi (where I am from). It took me a while to learn this, but as I traveled the United States and the world, speaking my native tongue, I often got asked: "What do you mean?"

A friend of mine, an engineer from Maryland, tells of leading a design team at a construction site in South Carolina. One day, his lead designer, Darren, a hard-boiled man from New Bern, North Carolina, walked up and let loose this string of syllables.

"Jim-bob, Ima fixin' to curry these drawin's out to th' site an' let Jeff Hamm hold 'em."

My friend stared at Darren.

"You're gonna...what?"

Darren looked at him sternly and repeated the message, slower this time, like he was speaking to a toddler.

"Jim Bob, I'ma fixin'...to curry...these drawin's...out to th' site...and let Jeff Hamm hold 'em. Understan'?"

My friend shook his head.

"Darren, why are you *carrying* drawings anywhere? What are you *fixing*? Is something broke? Who is Jeff Hamm? And why does he want to *hold them*?"

That's when it dawned on Darren; he was caught in a cultural quagmire. Emphasizing each word for this poor, dumb Yankee, he managed to force out his message in a language any foreigner could understand:

"Jim, mah boss man. I'm ah plaaan-ing to take these here draaaw-in's to the construction fooorrre-man at the site—you know?

Where we's building? So that heee canna build whut we *dee*-signed. Is that aw-right wit' you?"

It all made sense now. North Carolina to Maryland by way of South Carolina, they finally managed to communicate and get the project completed. It's a good thing they weren't debating barbeque.

Now apply that lesson to a document recorded thousands of years ago and spanning vast cultures, with a lot more at stake than getting a polymer plant built, and you'll see why Jesus promised us Holy Spirit as a teacher before he left the earth. We need him!

3. WHAT DOES IT MEAN IN THEIR CULTURE?

We must ask ourselves: What did these words and/or actions mean to the people involved? See, we never learned this in Bible college or seminary. Instead, we were given the interpretation that best fit the perspective of the religious organization supporting the school. The fact is, most of the things we get from the Word of God are filtered through our Western culture—one that is foreign to the writers of the Bible.

Why is this important? Because we read through our ideology, then develop a philosophy, which eventually forms a belief system—some folks call this a worldview. This is why God must deal with our B.S. (it stands for Belief System) before he can lead us into greater truth. Remember Jesus' words:

> *No one sews a patch of unshrunk cloth on an old garment; otherwise, the patch pulls away from it, the new from the old, and a worse tear results. And no one puts new wine into old wineskins; otherwise the wine will burst the skins, and the wine is lost and the skins as well; but one puts new wine into fresh wineskins.*
>
> Mark 2:21-22

God will deal with our old wineskins, but only if we allow him to. This is not always pleasant. Yet we must constantly challenge our present reality, working with Holy Spirit to ask ourselves:

- Where are we?
- What are we doing?
- Why are we doing it?

In so doing, we allow ourselves to draw closer to the truth. In so doing, we'll find a lot that we must unlearn. Jesus told us that God's Word is truth. So then, out of our godly philosophy, we can develop a theology—how we relate to God.

4. How Do We Apply It to Our Lives?

The final act in processing truth is to apply it to our lives. But how? How do we bring new knowledge and experience to our lives and the lives of those we influence? How does the seed of truth grow?

When we bring truth into our lives, we cannot alter it. We cannot change it. We cannot say, "This is how it fits where I live." The gospel of the kingdom is not fluid; it is set in stone. This is God's idea of who he is. And I think he has a pretty good idea of who he is. In fact, his idea is pretty cool.

So, as we study the Word, we are going to ask:
- Who is speaking?
- Who are they speaking to?
- What does it mean in their culture?
- How do we apply it to our lives?

This simple pattern applied to the study of the Bible will bring freedom and revelation to us. Therefore, let us seek to remove, bind and destroy the Western cultural filter we have allowed to filter the Word of God. We must come against our traditions that have made the Word of God ineffective and learn to embrace the complete truth of all that God has revealed to mankind.[1]

---

[1] This chapter is repeated (mostly) from my book *The Gospel of the Kingdom*, 2022.

2

Identity Shift

THE APOSTLE PAUL HAD A PROBLEM. As a devout Jew, a Pharisee of Pharisees, he viewed the Gentile world with deep apprehension. That was, until God whacked him upside the head, knocked him off his ass, and commissioned him to bring the Kingdom of God to the Greek and Roman cultures of his day.[2] That must have been quite an awakening. I can hear him now: *No problem, God. I've prepared my entire life to operate at the pinnacle of Judaism, so why not send me to the Gentiles, a people I know nothing about? Makes perfect sense. NOT!*

There he was, trying to convert the Romans, Galatians, Corinthians, and anyone else who would pay him any mind. And what did he have at his disposal? What would relate to these heathens? Certainly not the scrolls of the Torah. (And my books weren't out in Greek yet.) Then it dawned on him: He could teach the people from their own culture!

Turns out, the Greco-Roman culture of the day had a remarkable custom: adoption. But it was not the practice of taking in the family-

---

[2] Expositor's Greek New Testament: Acts 9:4 (Page 186 notes) Lewin, Farrar (so Hackett, and some early interpreters), have held that Saul, and at least, some of his companions were mounted, since Saul was the emissary of the high priest, and the journey would occupy some days. As the strict Jews, like the Pharisees, seldom used horses. Their belief is that Saul and some of his companions rode upon an ass or a mule, not a horse.

less among them. They actually adopted their own children.

If this sounds crazy, remember that the three major cultures reflected in scripture: Greek, Roman and Hebrew, are vastly different than Western culture. When studying scripture, we need to understand the cultures in which the particular passage was written, and we need to fully understand our own culture to appreciate the lens through which we view the world. Few people in Western culture have studied history. We are an increasingly ignorant population. We might know the backstory to the Yellowstone TV series or the batting order of the LA Dodgers in the 2020 World Series, but we don't know a Pharisee from a Sadducee, or a shofar from a saxophone.

In our study of the Kingdom of God, we are putting a knife to the influence of the spirit of religion. We are finally understanding the Kingdom of God...as God intended it. It's not what the 21st-century mind thinks it is. Our minds are shifting. Our hearts are opening. Recall our four questions; they help us understand the written word of God (logos) that reveals the living word of God (rhema).

CHILD, SLAVE, HEIR, ORPHAN

Given the cultural divide facing this former Pharisee, Paul's epiphany was astounding. Using the Roman custom of adopting their own sons, he explained to the Galatians the relationship between God and his Christian people.

> *Now I say, as long as the heir is a child, he does not differ at all from a slave, although he is owner of everything, but he is under guardians and managers until the date set by the father. So we too, when we were children, were held in bondage under the elementary principles of the world. But when the fullness of the time came, God sent His Son, born of a woman, born under the Law, so that He might redeem those who were under the Law, that we might receive the adoption as sons and daughters. Because you are sons, God has sent the Spirit of His Son into our hearts, crying out,*

Identity Shift

"Abba! Father!" Therefore you are no longer a slave, but a son; and if a son, then an heir through God.

However at that time, when you did not know God, you were slaves to those which by nature are not gods.

Galatians 4:1-8

It's important to understand the definition of *slave* in the culture of the Galatians. Obviously, the term *slave* is abhorrent to people today. I'm from Mississippi, where memories of the tragic past are still raw. In this passage, however, Paul is not referring to the harsh treatment of captive people. From an age two millennia ago, to a culture already ruled under the oppression of imperial Rome, the definition of slave is better understood as a bondservant or indentured servant—a person who voluntarily placed themself in the service of others for a specified time period and for an agreed-upon outcome. This could be those who were paying off a debt, as well as lifelong servants who became engrafted into the family. The Apostle Paul often referred to himself as a bondservant or slave to the Lord. We do not find scriptural support for chattel slavery—the ownership of humans as property.

Now, considering the words *child* and *heir*, as we study adoption and sonship, we will learn that *child* also meant something different to biblical culture than it does today.

Look at verse 1, "Now I say, as long as the heir is a child, he does not differ at all from a slave, although he is the owner of everything."

The word *child* refers to age, as in "infant." It can also mean "simple-minded." But the root in the Greek means "immature person." Further, the word *heir* denotes the future stature of the child; it is comparable to *slave* in the sense that neither child nor slave has the rights of a full-grown son.

When we are born again, regardless of our social status, scripture says we become children of God. As we grow in God, we become sons of God, and thus heirs.

Therefore you are no longer a slave, but a son; and if a son, then an heir through God.

Galatians 4:7

Through our study, we will encounter scriptures that use the terms child, slave, heir and orphan somewhat interchangeably. In modern times, each word carries a vastly different connotation. Orphan, in our usage, indicates a relationship to Father God—specifically, the lack of one. Its meaning will become clearer as we progress.

ABOUT GENDER

Now, as we continue our discussion on Paul's teaching, we also need to address the elephant in the room. Specifically, we need to decide if the elephant is male or female. On the one hand, the word *son*, as recorded in Galatians, has nothing to do with gender. On the other hand, it has everything to do with gender. Let me explain.

The word *son* in Galatians 4 comes from the word *man*, which comes from *Adam*, which is "mankind." It means: "attendant, one who attends, a man, mature, to partner." *Son* comes from the word *Adam*, which speaks of the human race, i.e., mankind.

Recall that the man Adam was eventually separated into two genders: masculine (Adam) and feminine (Eve). As such, he would never be complete without her, and she would never be complete without him. As it turns out, the two of them together made quite a mess of things in the Garden, but that's another story.

Thus, the word *son*, as Paul used it, is gender-neutral. However, Paul was writing to a male-dominated society about an adoption practice involving fathers and sons. (No mention is made of any such ceremony for females.) However, it is telling that, in the same letter, Paul drew from the Greco-Roman custom of adoption to illustrate our relationship with God. He qualified it with these words:

Identity Shift

> *For all of you who were baptized into Christ have clothed yourselves with Christ. There is neither Jew nor Greek, there is neither slave nor free, <u>there is neither male nor female</u>; for you are all one in Christ Jesus. And if you belong to Christ, then you are Abraham's descendants, heirs according to promise.*
>
> Galatians 3:27-29

"Neither male nor female." It's as if he said: "I'm going to talk about sons and fathers in this example, but please don't go astray. It pertains to everybody."

Over the centuries, however, the word *son* evolved in the church's vocabulary to be primarily associated with masculinity or the male species. And it made perfect sense…to those in power. The church leadership was men. Local congregations were led by men. Where was the impetus for change? Yet for every man who read "son" as male and thought: *that makes perfect sense*, there was a woman of God who thought: *well, that sucks!*

Compounding the issue is the translation of God as "Father." The truth is, God is not exclusively male nor female. The Hebrew word for Father is, "the Source." It does not mean we are wrong to call God "Father" or "Daddy." It just means our definition is incomplete. There is a mother side to God's heart as well as a father side. We see this throughout scripture.

> *Can a woman forget her nursing child*
> *And have no compassion on the son of her womb?*
> *Even these may forget, but I will not forget you.*
> *Behold, I have inscribed you on the palms of My hands;*
> *Your walls are continually before Me.*
>
> Isaiah 49:15-16

But we proved to be gentle among you. As a nursing mother tenderly cares for her own children, in the same way we had a fond affection for you and were delighted to share with you not only the gospel of God, but also our own lives, because you had become very dear to us.

1 Thessalonians 2:7-8

Jerusalem, Jerusalem, the city that kills the prophets and stones those who have been sent to her! How often I wanted to gather your children together, just as a hen gathers her young under her wings, and you were unwilling!

Luke 13:34

I once heard a prominent woman minister—one who leads many people in the Kingdom of God—call herself a "Fathering leader." It made me sad. Was there no word in our language to capture the complete essence of God?

I realize I'm not going to change centuries of convention in these few pages. That's not our scope. Likewise, Paul was not out to address directly the host of issues plaguing the societies in which he ministered. He was, however, passionate to bring the Kingdom of God to all people—Jews, gentiles, slaves, free, men, women—for he knew that the evils they practiced were rooted in the fundamental power of sin.

I share his desire. This study is about the Kingdom of God, of orphans and mature ones, regardless of gender. To that end, I will use "sons and daughters" wherever possible, and occasionally use *sons* to imply both genders. Please allow the language—imperfect as it is—to convey the love of God as he matures all his children into the Kingdom of God.

ADOPTION BY GOD

God's adoption is "so that He might redeem those who were under the Law, that we might receive the adoption as sons and daughters" (Galatians 4:5). We could just as easily paraphrase this: "that we might receive the adoption of *the mature ones.*"

This word *adoption* in Western culture refers to an orphan, someone without a family, no parents, no home and no inheritance. They might be living in a children's home. They might be living on the streets. They might be looking for somebody to say, "Hey child, I want to take you home with me. I'm going to adopt you."

That is our western mindset of adoption. But in the culture of this scripture, it was different. Notice verse one: "as long as the heir is a child…." This gives us insight into who the child is; he's an heir, albeit an immature one. The word *immature* means "orphan or slave." As such, it deviates from the Western thought that an orphan is parentless. So, the word *child* means, "being immature, simple-minded, an infant or orphan." He has an inheritance; he has something awaiting his maturity, something he can partake of in his life. Yet at present, he's no different from a slave even though he's the future owner of everything.

Now, a child had no ownership in the father's house. They were orphans in the sense that they were not of the family lineage. Why is this important? Because religion today offers the same orphan mentality. Religion makes us feel that we don't belong in the father's house. Religion is wrong. God's word says:

> *Because you are sons, God has sent forth the Spirit of His Son into our hearts, crying, "Abba! Father!"*
>
> Galatians 4:6

> *For you have not received a spirit of slavery leading to fear again, but you have received a spirit of adoption as sons and daughters by which we cry out, "Abba! Father!"*
>
> Romans 8:15

THE CULTURE OF KINGDOM IDENTITY

Your identity determines the quality of your walk with God. If you don't know who you are, you cannot do what God has created you to do. If you have a childlike mentality—if you remain immature—you will live feeling unworthy and that you have no power in your life to overcome all that oppresses you. Poor habits will grow powerful and control you. Even though you are born-again—even if the Spirit of God dwells in you—the release of his power within you and beyond you will be severely limited. Your spiritual life will be stunted.

Galatians 4 compares the process to sonship. We start out as a child, (even though we own everything in name only), and we progress into maturity.

Religion, on the other hand, casts us as unworthy and that our place is in striving to do our best to make it to heaven. Religion forms us to live in fear, and if you live in fear, you cannot receive the love of God the Father. Religion offers an image of God as this grouchy old guy up in heaven with a long white beard and a stick in his hand, ready to whack us every time we mess up. That is not the Father of the Bible. That is not the God I serve.

The Bible tells us our Father is a loving God. He will correct us if we need it, but he's not focused on finding every fault, highlighting every shortcoming, and beating us to teach us a lesson. That is not in the Bible. Yet religion has brought us to the place where we believe God is perpetually angry at us because we cannot live up to his standards. The word of God tells us that he who is in us is greater than he who is in the world (ref. 1 John 4:4). He says we can do all things through Christ who gives us strength.

> *You are from God, little children, and have overcome them; because greater is He who is in you than he who is in the world.*
>
> 1 John 4:4

> *I have given you authority to tread on serpents and scorpions, and over all the power of the enemy, and nothing will injure you.*
>
> Luke 10:19

Identity Shift

Every person alive knows some pain. We know what it is like to be opposed, to be mistreated. Sometimes it's simply physics, like falling from a bicycle. Other times, it's outright oppression like an abusive spouse or a toxic work culture. Sometimes the foe is sickness, crop failure, or a failing economy. The fact is, we live in a rebellious world. Romans 5:12 tells us:

Therefore, just as through one man sin entered into the world, and death through sin, and so death spread to all mankind, because all sinned.

Here is the good news: our standing as sons and daughters of God is not determined by how we feel. It is not determined by how we wake up in the morning. Some people are frustrated with their relationships, dreading their jobs, and raging at the insanity in the world. Yet they are still married (happily!), still working (profitably), and still in this world (hopefully). Just because they wake up feeling one way doesn't change who they really are. That is the way of a son or daughter of God. It is not based on our feelings; it is based on our standing. It is based on God's word.

Religion teaches us to live in condemnation. The power of condemnation comes when we believe it; we actually think we deserve it. (In fact, the power of anything is in our believing it.) Well...we don't deserve condemnation. Do we make mistakes? Certainly. Is God's correction intended to vent his wrath on us? No. His correction is to set us right, lift us from the pavement when we fall, tend our wounds, teach us to fight back, train us to stand, and most of all: condition us to rebuke the enemy by loving ourselves. We learn to live this verse:

Therefore, there is now no condemnation for those who are in Christ Jesus.

Romans 8:1 NIV

Religion teaches us to live life by a yardstick—what is right and what is wrong. Yet that is not the nature of relationship. We should live by what is life and death. Now, I'm not saying there isn't a right and a wrong, a good and an evil. I'm saying that the determinant is what brings life and what brings death. Note God's declaration to the newly emancipated children of Israel. After uttering warning upon warning, plea upon plea, God's word to his beloved people came down to this crucible moment, joining God's heart to their hearts.

> *I call heaven and earth to witness against you today, that I have placed before you life and death, the blessing and the curse. So choose life in order that you may live, you and your descendants.*
>
> Deuteronomy 30:19

God did not say: "Do right and don't do wrong." Sure, he outlined right and wrong, but what is that but a means to an end, the goal being life or death. Spiritual growth to sonship is not a matter for a yardstick. It's a matter for the living word of God.

People come to me everywhere I go, wanting to know if I believe such and such is right or wrong. "Greg, do you believe drinking alcohol is right or wrong? Do you believe this lifestyle is wrong or that doing this thing is wrong? Do you believe, if somebody slips up and does this <insert your favorite sin>, it is right or wrong?"

I've learned to answer thusly: "You are asking the wrong question. It is not whether I believe it is right or wrong or not, nor whether you believe it is right or wrong. What does God say about it? Because when we do that, that changes everything, because in the kingdom, you have no opinion on what is right and wrong."

See, when we operate out of the condemnation of religion, we conform out of fear—the fear of God's inspection of our lives leading to the certainty of his wrath. But when we realize he loves us, that love permeates everything we experience with him, and we want to conform. It is our heart's desire, and so we operate out of love. Living out of a sense of right and wrong cannot change behavior any more than a barometer changes weather. God's love changes everything it reaches. That's the point where his word, his will, his authority and his standards become meaningful because they reach our hearts.

Identity Shift

*Even though I walk through the valley
of the shadow of death,
I fear no evil, for You are with me;
Your rod and Your staff, they comfort me.*

Psalm 23:4

America is a republic, not a democracy. A republic is governed by law. A democracy is governed by the majority of the people. As a republic, America is governed by law. In a kingdom, the king's word is law. In America, we get to voice an opinion every two years about our congress. We go to the voting booth and choose. Every six years we get to do that with our senators, and every four years, we are able to do that with our president.

Kings, however, are not voted in. They are not even appointed. They are crowned. They are kings by inherent right. The throne is theirs because it has always been in their family, or they took it from another family (while claiming it through a branch of ancestry). Regardless of how they arrived, they rule by the familial right of kings. I'm a king because...I am.

OUR GOVERNOR

As kingdom Christians, we are not called to be religious people. We are called to be kingdom people. Our identity derives from who we are in the family of God. Religion paints a dreary picture of our identity. *If you didn't do right this week, God is mad at you. If you thought wrongly about somebody this week, God's out to get you.* That is religion.

> We need God to shift our culture because culture dictates morals.

Here is the good news. There is this wonderful person who lives within every born-again believer: Holy Spirit. When we go astray, he's there to convict us, reprove us, nudge us, and set us straight. He guides us, but not into moral standards. Rather, he guides us into a new culture called kingdom culture. Trying to live morally in a religious atmosphere doesn't work. We don't need God to fix our morals. We need God to shift our culture because culture dictates morals. Religion sets standards; they are morally sound but impossible to attain. Kingdom establishes our real identity as sons and daughters of God. When our identity shifts, God's moral standards become part of us—they are in our DNA. God has called us to living sonship according to the Kingdom of God.

Now, I mess up at times. My wife, Joan, can make you a list. Please don't ask her for it. She'll sell it to you. She's got copies printed up with pictures, dates and times. She knows I'm not perfect. My friends know I'm not perfect. I know it too…but that doesn't affect who I am in Christ. I am a son of God. We are sons of God. Ladies, you are sons of God. If a man can be a bride, you can be a son. Hallelujah.

In my previous book, *The Gospel of the Kingdom*, I discussed the contrast between the Gospel of the Kingdom and the Gospel of Salvation. Salvation gets you in the door, but that's as far as you get! I know people who have been believers for 40 years and they're still children. They have been in church most of their lives, yet they cling to a child's immature, simple-minded identity because they do not allow Holy Spirit to govern them.

The word *govern* means "to regulate." God wants to govern us. He is the governor of our lives. However, God doesn't want to control us. He is not the author of everything that happens to us. Yes, it is comforting to think that God controls everything that happens in the world. We envision him conducting us down the highway of life, orchestrating every other car sharing the road around us. We imagine him steering us from potholes, moving us to the fast lane when a semi is broken down up ahead. Yes, we think, God knew that semi would breakdown at that exact spot, at this specific time. He knew it from the beginning of all time, and so we are safe.

Safe…until a jerk in a red convertible cuts us off, flips the bird and brake checks us, sending scalding coffee into our laps as we scream things no Christian should utter, let alone imagine. It's at that moment when we might question our tidy theology and speculate on the random nature of life as it pertains to man's freewill. But we don't, of course. We're too busy renouncing the idiot's ancestry on his mother's side while tracing his roots all the way back to the Neanderthals.

The stark truth is that God doesn't control us, not as orphans nor as sons. The good news is that he governs us—he guides us, leads us, at times, carries us. But he doesn't control us.

Consider a gasoline or steam engine. There is a device called a governor. Its job is to regulate engine speed. Simple and ingenious, it lowers the throttle position when the speed is too high, and it raises the throttle position when the speed is too low. It is not the engine, nor is it the fuel. It is the regulator. Without it, the engine would die at low speed or blow apart at high speed. It is the mechanical guardian of the machine's inner workings. God, in the form of Holy Spirit, is the spiritual guardian of our inner workings. He works through our free will. We follow him to our blessing. We ignore him at our peril. We figure things out quickly.

RESTORED AND REDEEMED

In Galatians 4, Paul refers to the date that a child emerges as a son or daughter:

> *Now I say, as long as the heir is a child, he does not differ at all from a slave, although he is owner of everything, but he is under guardians and managers until the date set by the father.*
>
> Galatians 4:1-2

The date? Set by whom? *The Father.* So, this orphan—this heir who owns everything but cannot touch any of it—is being watched by his father who will set a date to adopt him.

Now, religion says that when we get born again, we are adopted. Yet that is not scriptural. When we are born again, it is not an adoption; it is a returning home; becoming engrafted in. It is coming back to our Father's house. We are no longer homeless; we are no longer fatherless; we now have an inheritance. We were lost, living in a nation that we were not designed to live in: the Kingdom of Darkness. When we find our Father and give our lives to him, it is not an adoption. Rather, it is a return, a restoration to what God originally intended us to be.

The Bible says those who have accepted Jesus Christ as their Lord and Savior are restored to the relationship he intended before the fall. Now, I'm not an English teacher—I butcher the English language quite gloriously—but when a word starts with "re," it means "to do it again." To be restored, therefore, means we have been put back into store. Likewise, we've been redeemed. That means we've been deemed again. So, salvation does not connect us to God for the first time. We, as humans, were God's sons and daughters before sin came into the world and messed everything up. Salvation restores and redeems better than before!

> Then God said, "Let Us make man in Our image, according to Our likeness; and let them rule over the fish of the sea and over the birds of the sky and over the cattle and over all the earth, and over every creeping thing that creeps on the earth." God created man in His own image, in the image of God He created him; male and female He created them. God blessed them; and God said to them, "Be fruitful and multiply, and fill the earth, and subdue it; and rule over the fish of the sea and over the birds of the sky and over every living thing that moves on the earth."
>
> Genesis 1:26-28

We are created in the image of God. Through salvation, we are brought back to God's original intent: for us to share his glory, his power and his fellowship. We are restored to the place where we left off as children in the Garden. The child is the simple-minded one, the immature one, the orphan. She's no different than a bondservant, even though she owns everything. She is destined for an inheritance...but not yet.

> God doesn't want us to squander our inheritance.

Most people plan to leave their children an inheritance. And why not? When they are four years old, we still like them. When they are eight, it's different. We still love them, but we might not like them. When they get to be 13 and 14, oh man…. We wouldn't give our four-year-old son or daughter the car keys and send them to the store for milk. That would be irresponsible. Likewise, God is not going to take things from our inheritance and put them in our hands when we are not ready to handle them.

That is why many people today are frustrated. They know God has things for them; they know they have an inheritance. Yet God is not releasing it to them. Could it be that they are not mature enough to handle it? God doesn't want us to squander our inheritance. Sure, the prodigal son was restored back to the father's house, but that's not where the story ends. We don't see the years he worked for his father, restoring from the inside what he wasted on the outside.

GUARDIANS

Consider verse 2 of Galatians 4. "But he [the child] is under guardians and managers until the date set by the father." The word *guardian* means "an administrator." The word *manager* is the word *oikonomos,* and it means, "one who manages or stewards." The guardian for us today is Holy Spirit, and the managers are the fivefold ministry. They steward us and grow us into sons and daughters of God.

The fivefold ministry gifts of Ephesians 4 are to steward the Body of Christ to maturity "until we all attain to the unity of the faith, and of the knowledge of the Son of God, to a mature man, to the measure of the stature which belongs to the fullness of Christ (Ephesians 4:13)."

From Ephesians 4:7-16, we know that the fivefold giftings are the apostles, prophets, evangelists, pastors and teachers. They're still active in the body of Christ; none of them have ceased operating. Paul's letter to the Ephesians tells us why the gifts were given and what they do in the life of the saints. Notice that nothing is said about preparing us to go to heaven. That is because God's goal is not to get us to heaven. God's goal is to get heaven into the earth. Jesus' prayer in Matthew 6:9-10 makes that clear:

> *Our Father who is in heaven,*
> *Hallowed be Your name.*
> *Your kingdom come.*
> *Your will be done,*
> *On earth as it is in heaven.*

There is much to be understood from this passage. Jesus is instructing his disciples (and by extension, us) in the way that they should pray. I know many Christians call this The Lord's Prayer, but it really should be The Disciples' Prayer.

Notice in scripture that whenever Jesus referred to the Father, he usually included the Father's location: "Our Father who is in heaven." (This will become more important in later chapters.)

Remember, God's Holy Spirit flows best when our prayers align with our purpose, specifically our assignment. Following Jesus' example, we first pray for the Kingdom of God to come and the will of God to be done on earth as it is in heaven. This highlights the differences between religion and kingdom. Religion focuses on heaven. Kingdom focuses on earth.

With regard to prayer, religion says God responds to our pleading. Kingdom says God responds to our faith—that which flows from our absolute conviction that he is a God who will manifest in our midst as we flow in harmony with his purpose for our lives. It's not like he ignores us; he doesn't. Our prayers might get answered; we might get what we asked for; but if our asking is askew of our calling in God, the answers will not meet our real needs.

Identity Shift

Think of it this way: there are many instruments in an orchestra: stringed instruments, woodwinds, drums and brass. Well, what happens when the trumpets look around and see the violas flirting with the majestic double bass violins standing in the back? They decide they want to be basses too. And since the bass violins use large bows to produce those thunderous notes, the trumpets start praying: "God, we need bows. Send us bows. Oh God, why doest thou ignorest our needeth? We shallest perseverest to the endeth, O' Lord God! Test us and provest useth, O' Father. Make us worthy of bows."

Problem is—trumpets don't need bows. They need wind. Why? Because they're trumpets! James, who had far less imagination, put it this way:

You ask and do not receive, because you ask with the wrong motives, so that you may spend what you request on your pleasures.

James 4:3

At first glance, this admonishment sounds like we're praying for a wild weekend in Vegas, but really, the key phrase is: "wrong motives." Wanting to be something that violates your true calling is a wrong motive. It doesn't mean you're evil; it just means you're wrong. Being wrong doesn't mean God doesn't love you, won't answer you or provide for you. It just means you aren't in line to receive God's best. I have known many a person who received from God what they asked for, only to limp along trying to be something they clearly were not meant to be. The trumpets in our example might get their bows, but they'll never play those deep throbbing notes, and the violas will still be into the basses. That's just how it works. (Sorry trumpets.)

As we pray, our first query should be to seek God's will in our lives. This will be an ever-deepening pursuit. Listen: Run...do not walk...from anyone claiming to "have arrived." Answered prayers for God's will for our lives are meant to propel us; they sustain us for the journey. Seeking God's will to put a title on your business card or to shore up a faltering ego are wrong motives.

An orphan prays solely from elemental needs. A son or daughter prays from a sense of purpose, seeking to accomplish God's will in their life. Of course, everyone has elemental needs (and everyone starts as an orphan). The difference, however, is focus. Do we care more about our daily bread or acquiring a bakery?

Here is the key. In the midst of seeking our purpose, our calling, our reason for this marvelous relationship restored by salvation, we will come across situations that drive us to our knees. Our souls will cry out in agony for the starving child, the family on drugs, the bankrupt missionary outreach, the corrupt government, the world on the brink of destruction. We will pray for no other reason than we see a need and are desperate for God to intervene. And therein lies our answer, my friends. While we are busy asking God to tell us our purpose, he is busy showing us our purpose.

Do not shy away from elemental prayers. Instead, be ready when they reveal our deeper calling. This is how orphans become sons and daughters.

PROJECT EARTH

Our present assignment is not heaven; it is earth. Yes, scripture says those who are born again go to heaven, but our gifts are intended to bring heaven to earth. Mankind did not fall from heaven when we sinned. We fell from dominion—the dominion of the earth. Religion has twisted our reality, making our entire hope that we will be extracted from this wretched world and ensconced safely in the billowy folds of heaven. Unfortunately, this is unscriptural, and it promotes false hope. (What's a billowy fold, anyway?) The truth is this: heaven is coming to earth. "Your kingdom come. Your will be done." Nothing in Jesus' prayer says: "Rescue us from this veil of tears." God intends to establish his kingdom here.

Focusing on heaven distorts our identity. It makes us weak, unimportant, worthless. We are reduced to beggars holding out a hand to angelic passersby as we await the flaming chariot to whisk us

Identity Shift

to glory land. Folks, we are not powerless. We are not impoverished spectators reduced to passive waiting. We are children of God, maturing to sons and daughters, taking our part in the establishment of the Kingdom of God.

> We are not impoverished spectators reduced to passive waiting. We are children of God.

There is a reason I named my university Kingdom University and not Heaven University. We will go to heaven when our time on earth is through. We understand that, but Jesus never insinuated that God's purpose was to get us into heaven. Rather, through us, we are bringing heaven into the earth.

Western religious culture focuses on utopia, something better to get us out of a tough spot, a bad life, horrible circumstances. Let us remind ourselves that scripture says: "You are from God, little children, and have overcome them; because greater is He who is in you than he who is in the world" (1 John 4:4). Sure, tough times come, sometimes overwhelming us in grief and despair. Yet the truth of scripture is sure: "But in all these things we overwhelmingly conquer through Him who loved us" (Romans 8:37).

For our circumstances to shift, our identity needs to shift into what Father has for us. We cannot afford to have a thought in our head about ourselves that God doesn't have in his head about us. Weakness comes as we believe weak things and live outside the power of our true identity in Christ.

In Mark 16, Jesus identified the five things that shall follow those who believe in him:

- they will cast out demons
- they will speak with new tongues
- they will pick up serpents
- if they drink any deadly poison, it will not harm them
- they will lay hands on the sick, and they will recover.

Now please, don't go hunting snakes or guzzling arsenic to prove you're holy. Jesus also said: "You shall not put the Lord your God to the test." These promises are for when we need them. Paul was bitten by a viper in front of unbelieving natives. He calmly shook it off into the fire. Guess what? The natives decided he was from God.

Guardians and managers have been put into our lives to mature us to where we are actually sons and daughters of God instead of children of God. When we are children of God, we think like this: *My dad will take care of me. My dad provides for me and protects me. He stands in front of me and he's always there for me. And one day, I'm going to go live with him forever in heaven.*

That is the mindset of a child of God. As an immature one, we always need Daddy to take care of us.

Now, I know what you're wondering: *You mean God's not going to take care of me forever?* No, he's not. God doesn't want to take care of us forever. I know it sounds strange, but it's true. Those of us who have grown kids: do they still show up hungry and raid our refrigerator every day? (No) Do they call to borrow money every day? (I hope not.) Do we still buy their clothes? No way! You think they'd be wearing ripped jeans if we were paying for them? When I was a boy, we threw jeans away when they got all tore up. Now, they sell for hundreds of dollars!

As our children mature into adulthood, our relationship with them evolves to the point where we are friends; they are no longer our babies, and we are no longer their babysitters. What matures them? Well...we matured them; responsibilities matured them; life matured them. In similar manner, Holy Spirit has been put in our lives to govern and mature us.

Romans 8:14 says: "For all who are being led by the Spirit of God, these are the sons of God." Not the children of God, but the sons, men and women, the mature ones of God. When we are born again, Holy Spirit comes back into our lives to govern us, to lead and guide us. Fear is not our guide. Sickness and disease are not our guides. Holy Spirit is our guide. Who are "those that are led by the Spirit of God"? They are us, the sons and daughters of God.

> A king in a manger is still a king, but he has a lot to learn.

Have you ever watched the children of royalty? They walk perfectly, speak precisely, and manner impeccably. You think they were born that way? A king in a manger is still a king, but he has a lot to learn. Children of royalty—future kings and queens, nobles, lords and ladies—are raised surrounded by tutors and governors who teach them everything. Not just readin', 'ritin', and 'rythmatic; these kids are taught how to stand. Their teachers put books on their heads to perfect their posture. They learn how to eat at a formal dinner, how to greet people, when to bow and curtsey. Their governors groom them to be what their birthright says they are.

Just because we are born again into the Kingdom of God doesn't mean we know how to act like kings and queens. Holy Spirit teaches us that. Jesus didn't launch his ministry at birth, even though he was the Son of God.

The Bible says that we "have an anointing from the Holy One..." (1 John 2:20).

> *And as for you, the anointing which you received from Him remains in you, and you have no need for anyone to teach you; but as His anointing teaches you about all things, and is true and is not a lie, and just as it has taught you, you remain in Him.*
>
> 1 John 2:27

We have an unction within us; we need no man to teach us. We have Holy Spirit to teach us. He bears witness that the things we are hearing are the truth. Holy Spirit deposits this knowledge through governors: the fivefold ministry that imparts God's truth into our lives. We are learning to be royals. Peter called us a royal priesthood.

> *But you are a chosen people, a royal priesthood, a holy nation, a people for God's own possession, so that you may*

> *proclaim the excellencies of Him who has called you out of darkness into His marvelous light;*
>
> 1 Peter 2:9

We are not paupers; we are not orphans; although a few of us are court jesters. In the Kingdom of God, there are no second-class citizens. Everybody in the kingdom is a son or daughter. We are all family. The entirety of Daddy's Kingdom is family. The Greek word is *oikos*. We are made up of *oikos* family, and we are prepared to step into our kingdom purpose. This is why we are put under guardians and managers, as it says in Galatians.

> *But he is under guardians and managers until the date set by the father. So also you, while you were children, were held in bondage under the elemental things of the world.*
>
> Galatians 4:2-3

The word *manager* comes from *oikonomos*. It literally means, "to manage or to steward or to treasure." So, not only is the Holy Spirit in our lives, but God has set ministerial guardians in our lives—apostles, prophets, evangelists, pastors and teachers—to equip us to do the work of the ministry. The focus of this equipping is our adoption as sons and daughters.

THE EARTH AND THE WORLD

The Father is raising mature sons and daughters through identity; people who know who we are in God's kingdom. So, Father has set a date and says, while we were children, we were held in bondage under "the elemental things of the world."

Now, remember our four questions:
- Who's talking?
- Who are they talking to?
- What does it mean in their culture?
- How do we apply it to our lives?

Identity Shift

In this phrase: "held in bondage under the elemental things of the world," the Greek word *world* is *kosmos*. What does *kosmos* mean in the Greek? It doesn't mean the stars in the Milky Way. *Kosmos* means several things, among them: "order, government order, rulership or to rule within a structure." So, when we talk about *kosmos*, we are talking about order or governmental structure.

This presents a dilemma for Western Christians because the word *world* has been applied as a value judgment: *come out from among the world; don't live like the world, live like a believer.* World is associated with sin, and that is unfortunate because it doesn't mean sin at all. "Elemental things of the world" refers to a time when we were held in bondage to a governmental order or structure of which we are no longer a part.

Closely associated with this concept is the word *repentance,* or *to repent*. The word *repent* doesn't mean to come to Pastor Jim and tell him all our sins. That's confession, and it's good for the soul. Hallelujah! But the word *repent* to the Greek, Jew and Roman cultures meant: "to change the way that we think or to change the way that we relate to something."

Remember, we are talking about identity. We are talking about sonship according to the kingdom, not religion. When Paul used *kosmos* (translated "world"), he was saying a governmental order or structure held us in bondage. Why is this so important? Because there are only two governmental orders or structures on the earth: the Kingdom of Darkness and the Kingdom of Light. The word *kingdom* has to do with "governmental order." It has to do with, "to rule." So, we are not living by religious standards, we are living by the standards of a government.

The word *government* could pertain to a nation, a country or a kingdom. Each has its own culture. And as anyone who has traveled and been immersed into a foreign culture will tell you, when we step into a different culture, we are lost for a while. Now, mankind was not born for the Kingdom of Darkness. It is foreign to us. We were born for the Kingdom of Light; that is where we belong. When we come into the Kingdom of Light, we find joy, peace, hope and fulfillment. We find all of those things. Why? Because culturally, it is already in us, and now we identify with those things that were lost to our lives.

When we consider *kosmos* in the context of kingdom, we have two words: *king* and *dominion*, which means "to dominate or rule." So, *kingdom* is: "the sovereign rule or domination of a king." By *king*, we mean one who rules a specific territory. To rule implies authority. Kings cannot have kingdoms without authority over certain territory. In a geographical sense, this is land and sea, *terra firma* and *oceanus*. Humans were formed from the earth; thus, our kings mark their territory accordingly. God's kingdom is comprised of authority in all realms: natural and supernatural.

> *And Jesus came up and spoke to them, saying, "All authority has been given to Me in heaven and on earth. Go therefore and make disciples of all the nations, baptizing them in the name of the Father and the Son and the Holy Spirit, teaching them to observe all that I commanded you; and lo, I am with you always, even to the end of the age."*
>
> Matthew 28:18-20

God loves the nations, so much so that he tells us to go to every nation and teach them what we have learned about him. God loves countries; God loves the land. He created this big, blue marble, and he called it earth. He loves the earth. The Bible says, "the earth is the Lord's and the fullness thereof" (Psalm 24:1). The earth is part of our dominion as rulers in God's kingdom. We are not of the Kingdom of Darkness. We are of a different *kosmos*, a different governing order—the Kingdom of Light.

Patriots are those who love their country. I love my country (America), and I don't want anything to destroy it. Glory to God! The word *patriot* means "to buy in or to believe in the establishment set forth by the founders." As patriots of our countries, we buy into the ideologies and philosophies of our founders. As patriots of the

Identity Shift

Kingdom of God, we align with the ideologies and philosophies of our founder: our Father who is in heaven, the King of his Kingdom.

Now, before we charge the darkness illuminated with our dog-eared copies of the New Testament (red letter editions, of course), our kingdom relationship with God needs to be fully appreciated. We are often told by well-meaning teachers that we have a voice in the kingdom. Others say the only voice we have is "yes" or "no." What's the answer?

Scripturally, as kings and queens in God's kingdom, we do have a voice, though it is under his. Still, ours is a necessary voice. So many places in scripture, God was moved by people's opinion. Other places, he was not moved at all. I realize that Jesus said he only did what he saw the Father do, but…what did he see the Father do? The Father responded to Abraham's pleading to spare Sodom and Gomorrah. He responded to Moses' pleas to spare the children of Israel. He responded to Jesus' plea to forgive his murderers, "for they know not what they do."

Consider what Jesus said the night he was betrayed and apprehended:

> *And behold, one of those who were with Jesus reached and drew his sword and struck the slave of the high priest and cut off his ear. Then Jesus said to him, "Put your sword back into its place; for all those who take up the sword will perish by the sword. <u>Or do you think that I cannot appeal to My Father, and He will at once put at My disposal more than twelve legions of angels?</u>*
>
> Matthew 26:51-53

Clearly, Jesus had options on the way to the cross. Consider the Garden of Gethsemane. What does Jesus' surrender mean— "Not my will, but yours be done"—if the Father would not have honored Jesus' request to spare him?

In many other places in scripture, the offer is clear: *Ask and you shall receive.* We have a will and a voice. Indeed, we are encouraged to use them. Yet we are encouraged by the word of God...and his word is law. "The Law of the Lord is perfect, restoring the soul" (Psalm 19:7). Yes, the word of the king is law—even when, by law, we are told to exercise our will as sons and daughters of the King. And his law is binding.

That is how Daniel ended up in the lion's den (ref. Daniel 6). King Darius did not want to throw Daniel into the pit, but he was tricked into uttering that command. The king in that culture couldn't change his word.

The next morning, Darius ran to the edge of the pit and cried: "Daniel, did your God save you?"

"I'm fine," said Daniel. "The lions are fine. A bit hungry, but we're all fine. I'm climbing out, now. How about rounding up my fat, juicy accusers?"

In the Kingdom of God, the word of the King is law. When we give our lives to God, his word becomes law in our life, not to bind us, but to restore us back into our original identity.

> But when <u>the fullness of the time</u> came, God sent forth His Son, born of a woman, born under the Law, so that He might redeem those who were under the Law, that you might receive the adoption as sons.
>
> Galatians 4:4-5

That's an interesting phrase: "the fullness of time." God was looking for a perfect time to bring forth his son into the earth so we who were born under the law could be redeemed from the law. That perfect time was 2000 years ago when Rome ruled the Middle East. The Roman kingdom resembled God's kingdom. Make no mistake, they were ruthless and merciless conquerors. But their governance model was close to what God had in mind—not the way they treated people, nor the way they conducted themselves morally, but their governing structure.

The time was right, and God sent Jesus to the earth.

3

Family Business

LIKE A WELL-WRITTEN NOVEL, Paul's letter to the Galatians weaves an ever-tightening storyline of adoption in the Greek and Roman culture. The son of a family starts life as an immature and undeveloped child, practically an orphan, with no more rights than a bondservant. Yet he is an heir; he has a birthright. His father has an inheritance reserved for him, but the son can't touch it until he evolves into a man. To that end, he must submit to governors and managers. They give the son chores—gardening, cleaning, tending livestock. They teach him to be a wise steward. They train him as a member of a royal family. The father monitors the son's development with a calculating appraisal.

Based on reports from the guardians and his own observations, the father realizes the time has come. *Now I can trust my son. I can send him on journeys. He can assume authority over a region. This day, I'm going to adopt my son.*

Adoption was not religious to the Greeks and Romans. This was not a bar mitzvah. Paul used this example to differentiate from religious observances. In his letter to the Galatians, he wasn't speaking to Jews; he was speaking to pagans. Galatians understood adoption as practiced in the Greco-Roman culture. Paul was speaking to the home crowd. Even though the adopted child was the biological product of his mother and father, he wasn't considered a trusted son until he was adopted.

Here is how Bible scholar Thomas Overmiller describes it.

Adoption differs from what we call "adoption" today. It describes how a Roman parent would formally and legally acknowledge his son's promotion from child to adult. This promotion would end the intrusive micromanagement of guardians and entrust the child with adult-level responsibility, decision-making freedom, and access to the family estate.

This kind of "adoption" could involve two kinds of people.

- A man's actual, biological children. They would be "adopted" as adult sons when the father determined they were ready.

- Someone outside the immediate or biological family, like our adoptions today. This would occur when a father acknowledged a faithful slave, the son of a friend, or some other person as an adult participant in his estate.

Perhaps the most famous Roman adoption is when Julius Caesar adopted Augustus Caesar. Augustus was a great-nephew to Julius and since Julius had no heir to the position of Caesar and no inheritor for his will, he adopted Julius as his son at eighteen years of age. This practice occurred other times as well, when a Roman emperor approached the end of his life with no heir, he would adopt an adult man whom he believed would rule well in his place.

This arrangement helps us understand what Paul is saying here. Both Jews (biological descendants of Abraham) and non-Jews (outside observers) received the blessing of a right relationship with God through faith in Christ, not through obeying the law. We're not just "added to God's family" so to speak, but we're recognized as responsible, trustworthy adults whom God desires to manage his resources and carry out his will on his behalf.[3]

THE CEREMONY

Here's how the adoption ceremony would proceed.

The father summons all of the city: the leaders, the merchants, the families and bondservants, and the entire immediate family. He brings them into one place, stands on a pedestal with his arm around his son. He pulls his son in tight so there's no gap between them. Then he makes decrees to the entire population gathered to witness the event.

"I declare this day that I adopt my son. He has become a partner in the family business. When he speaks, he speaks for me. When he conducts business, it is in our name. Whatever he owes you is my debt. Whatever I owe you is his debt. When he deals with others, it is our dealings. My son is no longer a dependent. He is a partner. He bears the family name. He is now a rightful heir."

The father then gives him a new robe, a ring, and a pair of sandals. Hallelujah![4]

---

[3] https://shepherdthoughts.com/baptistchurchny/adopted-as-sons-and-heirs

[4] The Greek word: *Huiothesia* (adoption) is formed by combining *huios* (son) and *thesis* (a placing) and literally means "the placing as a son" or "adoption."
In the Greek world the word is found only as early as the second century B.C.; however, the concept of adoption (place a son) is much earlier. In Crete (fifth century B.C.) adoption had "to take place on the market-square before the assembled citizens and from the speaker's tribunal."
Gerald Cowen, https://www.sermonindex.net/modules/articles/index.php?view=article&aid=33490 ©2002-2023 SermonIndex.net Promoting Genuine Biblical Revival.

CHRISTIANS TODAY

This is the model Paul used to describe our adoption as sons and daughters of God. In a general sense, this is how we mature from dependents to partners. When we partner with God, we share in everything he owns. What's his is ours, and what's ours is his. No longer a child with an immature mindset, we emerge from our orphan mentality. We gain access to our inheritance as God releases it to us.

Now, the question in anyone's mind should be: *OK, I was born again. So, when am I adopted by God?* The answer is, *like* the Galatians, our adoption process is gradual. As we mature, the Father releases more responsibility to us. Rather than crowning us with a single, momentous ceremony, the Father develops us in stages marked by prophetic words, revelations, baptisms, activations and assignments. In a sense, we experience a series of ceremonies. The closer we grow to God's heart, the more we grow into sonship and the more involved we become in the family business. God's heart, like ours, opens in degrees. While his love knows no bounds, our experience of that love is a life-long journey.

Remarkably, this was a journey that even Jesus experienced. In the gospel of Luke, we are told: "And Jesus kept increasing in wisdom and stature, and in favor with God and people" (Luke 2:52). Think about it. If I say I'm increasing in something, doesn't that mean that what I had yesterday is less than what I'll have tomorrow? Here, we are told that Jesus increased in favor with God. So, at one time he had less, and later, he had more.

Folks, religion would tell you that Jesus had carte blanche with heaven from the moment he arrived. Kingdom, however, will tell you different. Jesus soiled diapers and cut teeth and probably skinned a few knees on his way to becoming the sinless Lamb of God. He was a rabbi.

As we mature, we return home. We come back to family. We realize our inheritance. We grow into a place where we can operate in the family business. Our Father's business is not carpentry, not

> We are not here to make converts, because converts only seek heaven. We are here to make disciples, because disciples make history. We are history makers.

accounting, not baking, not truck driving or even ministry. Our heavenly Father is a King, and our family business is kingdom.

As we do business on the earth, we will do different things in the kingdom, but we are kings doing those things. We are not on earth to make a living. We are here to bring life to all we do. We need to see ourselves as kings. We are not sinners saved by grace, hanging on by a prayer, trying to make it to heaven the best way we can. That is religion. God calls us kings. Peter calls us "a royal priesthood." Jesus is the King of kings and Lord of lords, and we are of his lineage.

Our family business is kingdom, not religion. Everywhere we go, we are to bring kingdom, not religion. We are not here to make converts, because converts only seek heaven. We are here to make disciples because disciples make history. We are history makers.

The weakness in Christianity is that we've been trying to live by the rules of religion, and this has derailed us. Indeed, it has condemned us. It has brought us into a place of doubt where we don't know if God loves us today or hates us tomorrow. It is a place of confusion, frustration, and ultimately futility.

Here's the good news. Religion ends now! Say it with me:

"I declare the power, the influence, and the manipulation of religion is broken off my life, my family and all I am assigned to."

Declare this broken off from your life in the name of Jesus. We are aligning with our kingdom assignment, and that starts with being sons and daughters of God. Our assignment is not to be a good seamstress, doctor, electrician or teacher—whatever our occupation in life. Our assignment is to be a fully mature son or daughter. And out of that sonship, God gives us spheres of influence to steward for him in the Kingdom. We receive our metron—our area of influence, over which we carry God's authority. It is then that we become the seamstress, doctor, electrician or teacher for the kingdom. We are still sewing, mending, wiring and teaching, but we are doing it with a kingdom mindset, not a religious mindset.

Think about it: do you want a doctor who merely knows medicine? Or do you want a doctor whose Father created our bodies? Do you want drapes made by someone who merely knows cloth? Or do you want drapes crafted by hands that belong to the family of the priceless Lamb of God?

As we venture forth into the dark, lonely places of the world, we destroy the works of sin by the light of God, for we are of the Kingdom of Light. Our assignment is to call the kingdoms of this *kosmos*—the world—to become the Kingdoms of our God. Amen. Our assignment is not to win the lost—ours is not a lottery of human souls—but to call forth the sons and daughters of God, tell them they are living in the wrong country, and change their citizenship, starting with being born again. The cry of our lives is this: "Come in; come home; come back to the family of God; enter the Kingdom of Light."

Sound radical? Good. You're getting it. Now test it. Find any place in scripture where Jesus came to bring religion. Any place at all. (Here's a hint: it isn't there.) Now, some people read James 1:27.

Pure and undefiled religion in the sight of our God and Father is this: to visit orphans and widows in their distress, and to keep oneself unstained by the world.

Yes, it says "religion." King James had his translators use the word *religion* so the Church of England would have stronger rule of governance over the people. The actual word in the Greek means "service or ministry." Thus, we have a much better rendering of James 1:27: "Pure and undefiled *service* in the sight of our God...is this...." Jesus never came to give us religion. That was King James' idea. Fortunately, he's long gone, and now we need to bury his theology.

Jesus did not come to fix the Jewish religion. That was a common misconception in his day.

Family Business

> *So, when they* [the disciples] *had come together, they began asking Him, saying, "Lord, is it at this time that You are restoring the kingdom to Israel?"*
>
> Acts 1:6

Certainly, God loved the Jewish people. He still does. But his purpose in sending Jesus was not to restore the Jewish religion—or any religion, for that matter. Jesus brought revolution. The structure of the Jewish law was fulfilled, superseded and dismantled. Through Jesus, God restored his promise to Abraham—a kingdom, a priest! Hallelujah. Jesus gave us a kingdom. Establishing the Kingdom of God requires that we dismantle religion. Luke says it this way:

> *Do not fear, little flock, for it is your Father's good pleasure to give you the kingdom.*
>
> Luke 12:32 NKJV

This message echoes throughout the gospels. As we study, we'll see how we can displace the spirit of religion and step into the power of our true identity as God's sons and daughters.

In Paul's example to the Galatians, a father watched his son grow to the place of maturity, and then brought him in front of the whole community to declare him a partner in the family business, drawing him so close to him that there was no daylight between them. They were one. When you saw the son, you saw the father.

Jesus described something similar in defining his relationship with the Father to the Jewish leaders—ironically, the same Father God that the Jews purported to follow.

> *[The] Jews were seeking all the more to kill Him, because He not only was breaking the Sabbath, but also <u>was calling God His own Father, making Himself equal with God.</u>*
>
> John 5:18

Notice: by calling God his father, the Jews saw that as Jesus making himself equal with God. Isn't that exactly what Paul's model of adoption tells us? *This is my son. He speaks in my name. He operates in my name. We are partners. We are one and the same.*

Jesus described the relationship this way:

Therefore Jesus answered and was saying to them, "Truly, truly, I say to you, the Son can do nothing of Himself, unless it is something He sees the Father doing; for whatever the Father does, these things the Son also does in the same way. For the Father loves the Son and shows Him all things that He Himself is doing; and the Father will show Him greater works than these, so that you will be amazed. For just as the Father raises the dead and gives them life, so the Son also gives life to whom He wishes.

John 5:19-21

For I did not speak on My own, but the Father Himself who sent Me has given Me a commandment as to what to say and what to speak.

John 12:49

In his earthly ministry, Jesus did nothing except what was modeled for him by the Father. You saw Jesus; you saw the Father. We should do the same as we walk out our identity in the family of God. It is not always easy. We want to do things our way. That's fine for some things; not so fine for other things. There is a place where the stakes are so high, compared to our abilities, that complete surrender is the only way out; it is the only means possible of accomplishing all that God has given us to do.

Western culture hinders us in this regard. We are the rugged, self-reliant, pioneering types. We'd sooner die for our horse, a plug of tobacco, or the hand of a pretty girl than give our lives for the gospel. And yet, I have been in nations around the world where people actually do not love their life even unto death. They'll die for Jesus...and they frequently do.

Americans love God, but religion has made us comfortable in our padded pews and air conditioning. If something makes us uncomfortable, we go looking for another church that can make us more comfortable. Meanwhile, groups like the Islamic State sweep through the Middle East slaughtering Christians and leaving their leaders crucified on crude wooden crosses.

Paul understood this well.

That I may know Him and the power of His resurrection and the fellowship of His sufferings, being conformed to His death; if somehow I may attain to the resurrection from the dead.

Philippians 3:10

Yes, kingdom living is about the resurrection; it is about the power; it is also about the sacrifice. Our identity is found in Jesus, whose entire purpose on the earth was to restore the family, to provide a way to be born again, and to reestablish the Kingdom of God. He gave his life for it. Adam lost a kingdom. Jesus came to get a kingdom back.

So also it is written: "The first man, Adam, became a living person." The last Adam was a life-giving spirit.

1 Corinthians 15:45

THE CULTURE OF IDENTITY

Kingdom identity is not about living way out somewhere. It's not the young hero traveling to distant galaxies in search of his destiny and finding new friends along the way. It's happening right here, right now. The Kingdom of God is on the earth...and it's growing. The question is: Are we in the kingdom?

And Jesus was saying to them, "Truly I say to you, there are some of those who are standing here who will not taste death until they see the kingdom of God when it has come with power.

Mark 9:1

Amazingly, Jesus was saying: "Some of you folks right here with me, you're not dying until we see the Kingdom of God come in its power." Religion projects the Kingdom of God into the future through a convoluted eschatology involving the rescue of mankind from the cesspool of sinful earth.

Here's the good news: the Kingdom of God is now. It started 2000 years ago with the birth of Jesus. Yes, in one sense, Jesus was a baby like any other little guy. But in another sense, he was a king from the moment he stuck his head out, looked around, and thought: *Live barn animals! Cool!*

Do you think the Magi traveled for two years to see a mere baby? I'm sure they had babies in Magi-land. No, they weren't looking for Mary's little lamb. They were looking for a King, the King of the Jews, a king who had his own star. When they approached the regional despot, Herod, they asked him: "Where is he who has been born King of the Jews? For we saw his star in the east and have come to worship Him" (Matthew 2:2). Drawing from the Greek definition of the word *worship*, it is as if the Magi were saying: "We have come to bow before him and kiss his ring."

In hindsight, probably not the smartest move in the history of king-searching, for this inquiry had tragic results. Note, however, that the Magi didn't ask for a little lamb. They asked for a king. Herod became so paranoid that he gave orders to destroy every male child two years old and under. Yes...he killed two-year-olds. A baby doesn't threaten a king, but another king does.

Religion presents Jesus as an innocent lamb in swaddling clothes, his light-complected cheeks flush with innocence. In truth, he was royal born of the Father's DNA. Other kings brought gifts and bowed down to him. But instead of rattles and stuffed donkeys, they brought gold, myrrh and frankincense. Now, this wasn't three guys on camels like we see on Christmas cards. These kings traveled in caravans of hundreds of people. When they rolled up on Bethlehem spouting off about a new king, they were packing vast amounts of wealth and weaponry. They didn't bring Jesus a gold nugget they found at the river Jordan. They didn't bring a little bottle of anointing oil with a roller ball on top, labeled: "For Baby's First Intercession." No, they brought wealth—lots of it in large containers. History tells us they brought many more things than just these three gifts. This was a state visit to a king, a royal heir destined to take back the earth and establish the Kingdom of God. Jesus was the king sent to destroy the devil's works.

> *The one who practices sin is of the devil; for the devil has been sinning from the beginning. The Son of God appeared for this purpose, to destroy the works of the devil.*
>
> 1 John 3:8

Being a king is about being born into a royal family. It's about having a father as a king. It's about finding our purpose through that relationship. When we lack fathering, we have a tough time figuring out who we are. Our prisons today are full of young men who have no fathers. Growing up, their mothers were involved, but no man was in the home to help their sons grow into their identity.

The Son of God appeared with a purpose. He had an assignment—to destroy the works of the devil. The devil has been sinning from the beginning, all the way back to where the sinning started in Genesis 3. Adam and Eve made a deal with the devil in the Garden of Eden. When they fell, they did not fall from heaven; they did not fall from a religion. They fell from a dominion, from a kingdom. This is because man's first commission was one of dominion.

> *God blessed them; and God said to them, "Be fruitful and multiply, and fill the earth, and subdue it; and rule over the fish of the sea and over the birds of the sky and over every living thing that moves on the earth."*
>
> Genesis 1:28

The word translated "rule" is the Hebrew word *rada*, which means, "to have dominion or kingdom." God gave man dominion over every created thing on earth. It was the ability to rule over all created things.

> *Now no shrub of the field was yet in the earth, and no plant of the field had yet sprouted, for the Lord God had not sent rain upon the earth, and there was no man to cultivate the ground. But a mist used to rise from the earth and water the whole surface of the ground.*
>
> Genesis 2:5-6

In this passage, we understand that God was waiting for a man to tend the Garden. God did not allow any rain or growth of anything he created because there was not a man to manage it. He had no manager for the Garden. So, God created the atmosphere (the environment) and filled it with things, but he didn't push the START button for things to grow, flourish and be fruitful until he had a man to steward it. He needed a man to tend the garden.

Trouble started when Eve and the serpent began to commiserate about God's rules. "God doesn't want us to eat the fruit of that tree. He says we'll die. But it looks soooo good."

Of course, the serpent told them a lie that held a shred of truth: "You certainly will not die! For God knows that on the day you eat from it your eyes will be opened, and you will become like God, knowing good and evil" (Genesis 3:4-5). Next thing they know, they're naked and hiding from God, which was a shame, because God walked with them in the cool of the day. That phrase, "cool of the day," doesn't mean when the sun's coming or going. It means they walked with God in the spirit.

That is why, when they sinned, they did not lose a religion. There was no religious activity in the Garden. There were no altars, no worship bands, no skinny jeans, no preaching, prophesying, apostleship, pastors, or offering baskets. There was simply a government man named Adam (mankind) who was called a steward of the creation that God had created and called *kingdom*. When Adam and Eve fell, they lost a kingdom, not a religion.

When God gives us something, he gives us his original idea—the thing that was in his heart from the beginning. Religion has never been in God's heart. Religion has always been in the devil's heart. Lucifer wanted to be worshiped in a way that brought him glory. Our Father is different. He causes us to worship him because of the glory that he bestows upon us.

The fall of man was orchestrated by the devil in the Garden, and in 1 John 3:8, we understand that Jesus came to right that wrong. He came to destroy the works of the devil, "for the devil had sinned from the beginning. The Son of God appeared for this purpose, to destroy the works of the devil." Now, in our Bible, this word *works* is plural to the American eye. Religion teaches that *works* means, "drinking, smoking, dipping, chewing, swearing, and dating girls who do these things." Viewed in a religious light, *works* has come to mean all of these moral things that we do that we think are wrong. One might say that our assessment is guilt-induced. Thus, Jesus came to destroy the thing that we feel guilty about: rebellion.

Well, that is not what *works* means in the Greek. The Greek word is *ergon* or *argon*, and it means: "action, work singular, something that is effectual, task, and continual." It doesn't refer to many works; it means "one work that has continued." So, instead of all of these behaviors that arise from sin, 1 John 3:8 takes us back to the beginning where one work, *argon*, set in motion a growing world of sin over time. So, it is not works, as in many, that Jesus came to destroy, but one work that continues to operate—rebellion, that treasonous act.

In the phrase: "the Son of God appeared for this purpose," the word *appeared* is the Greek word *ephanerōthē*. It means, "to become visible or to make evident another's vision, to manifest another's vision, dream."

Thus, the Son of God was made clear, visible, evident, to make known someone else's vision. Whose vision was that? The Father's vision. Jesus didn't appear to do his own thing. He appeared to manifest the vision of the Father. What was the vision of the Father?

To get us all to heaven? No! (If you said *heaven*, send your book back. It's defective.)

Recall Genesis 3, in which Adam sinned and God read them the riot act! Still, have you ever wondered why God never intervened in that act? While Adam and Eve (actually, Eve and Adam) were messing up, why didn't God say, "Wait a minute! You can't eat that. Put it back. Spit it out!" We'd do that if we saw a toddler eating rat poison. Why didn't God take action? It's because God wasn't there in that sense. He removed himself from the authority structure in the earthly realm. That is why God needs us. God is not going to void his word and start over. From the beginning, he was clear where authority on earth rested:

> *Let Us make mankind in Our image, according to Our likeness; and let them rule over the fish of the sea and over the birds of the sky and over the livestock and over all the earth, and over every crawling thing that crawls on the earth.*
>
> Genesis 1:26

In the context of the Hebrew language, God pulled himself back and laid upon man the authority to govern, to establish governmental order in the *kosmos*, to rule over a *kosmos* kingdom, to *rada* in the earth.

Now, in this context, God's delegated authority was *on* the earth, but not *over* the earth. God never lost the earth. He lost the world. He lost the kingdom. The earth and the world are two different things. The Bible says that "the earth is the Lord's and the fullness thereof" (Psalm 24:1). That never changed. God lost dominion on the earth. He lost *rada*. He lost kingdom. But he kept the planet.

When Adam fell, God did not intervene directly, but the devil forgot God could talk. God prophesied his actions going forth:

Family Business

> *And I will put enmity*
> *between you and the woman,*
> *and between your offspring and hers;*
> *he will crush your head,*
> *and you will strike his heel.*
>
> Genesis 3:15 NIV

The crushed head of a serpent is a wonderful thing, don't you think? To better understand this, let's apply our third question to this passage. We know who said this (God). We know who they were saying it to (the devil). So, what did that mean in their culture? What did it mean when Moses wrote this? What did this mean to the Hebrews? Well, whenever a Hebrew baby was born, they held it up by the leg and slapped its heel, causing the baby to take in a sharp breath—the first of many (hopefully).

In inspiring this practice, God was reminding people of his decree in Genesis 3, that a deliverer was coming—the offspring of the woman—and he would crush the devil's head. (Interestingly, God did not say the offspring of the man.) This deliverer, fathered by God, would crush the serpent's head. The head represents authority. God was saying: "He's going to crush your authority when you strike his heel. You may take his breath, but his breath will only be interrupted; it will not be destroyed. When breath comes back into him—when he rises from the dead—he's going to crush your authority on the earth."

The word *woman* means "wombed man," or "man with a womb." This is man in the sense of mankind, so it could say "that part of mankind with a womb." Here, we see the providence of God. He created an entrance way into the earth before he needed it. He created woman so he could have a legal entry into the world after mankind messed up.

When God said, "It is not good for the man to be alone," he wasn't talking about Adam not having a mate like the other animals. He was saying that it is not good for man to be separated from his purpose and his destiny, which comes through Jehovah. It is not good for man to be alone. When we are without God, we are alone. We can be in a crowded room and be alone. We can be occupied with work and be alone. But when we are outside the environment that God created us to function in, we are outside of life itself.

> If we take man out of Eden—out of the presence and the atmosphere of God—he starts dying. Death reigns over him. Eventually he will die, and he will probably take others with him.

God always creates the environment before he creates the product. God created water before he created fish. God created sky before he created the bird. He created earth before he created plants, shrubs and trees. He created Eden before he created man. The word *Eden* means, "presence, atmosphere, environment." God set his presence in a place first, and then he put man in it. When we take a fish out of water, we take it out of its God-created environment. The poor fish will flop around on the bank for a while and finally give up and die. It can't live outside of the environment God created for it. When we take birds from the sky, they become vulnerable to land-based predators. If we take a tree or a bush out of the soil, it withers and disintegrates. Likewise, if we take man out of Eden—out of the presence and the atmosphere of God—he starts dying. Death reigns over him. Eventually he will die, and he will probably take others with him. "*For if by the offense of the one, death reigned through the one...*" (Romans 5:17).

We were created for God's presence. Adam sinned and surrendered his dominion. Thus, he was removed from Eden and the presence of God. Holy Spirit left the earth when Adam sinned, and he didn't return until Jesus' resurrection. Until the day of Pentecost, Holy Spirit never lived in anyone ('except Jesus, of course. Ref. Luke 4:1, Mark 5:30). Certainly, he came upon them for certain tasks, but he never made anyone his dwelling place. Adam sinned and lost a kingdom. Jesus manifested to get the kingdom back. His assignment was to bring the kingdom of God to earth. Coincidentally, that is our assignment as well.

> *He said to them, "Let us go somewhere else to the towns nearby, so that I may preach there also; for that is what I came for."*
>
> Mark 1:38

> *But He said to them, "I must preach the kingdom of God to the other cities also, for I was sent for this purpose."*
>
> Luke 4:43

In 1 John 3:8, where we are told Jesus appeared to "destroy the works of the devil," *destroy* is the Greek word *luo*. It means, "to loose, to release, to dissolve, to annul a contract." The connotation is to untangle us from something, to break us loose from agreements. Jesus was manifested for this purpose, that he might loose us from the contract we are tied to. Jesus didn't come just to get us into heaven. He came to untangle, unwrap and loose us from a bad deal that we were legally bound to, going all the way back to the Garden. Jesus came to perform a legal function, not a spiritual function nor a religious function. He came to nullify a legally binding contract. It was a governmental act—one government coming to another government and undoing something that an illegal government did. Glory to God!

SATAN'S PERSUASION

> *And he led Him up and showed Him all the kingdoms of the world in a moment of time. And the devil said to Him, "I will give you all this domain and its glory; for it has been handed over to me, and I give it to whomever I wish. Therefore if you worship before me, it shall all be yours." Jesus answered him, "It is written, 'You shall worship the Lord your God and serve Him only.'"*
>
> Luke 4:5-8

In the temptations of Jesus, the devil showed him all of the kingdoms of the world. "You can have it all," he said. With one catch. Notice what the devil *did not* use to tempt Jesus: the religions of the world. He knew Jesus did not come for religion; his was not a religious quest. It was a governmental quest. The devil showed Jesus the world in a moment's time because that's what Jesus came for.

Interestingly, the word *world* in this phrase is not the word *kosmos*. It is the word *homie*. (No, not your redneck friends.) It is from the word *oikos*, or *family*, meaning "those things that we've inhabited." So, the devil is literally saying here: "I am showing you all the kingdoms of your *oikos*, your family, in a moment's time."

The root word *oikas* could be interpreted as "family house." The devil was showing Jesus all of the kingdoms of his house—not the devil's house, but Jesus' house, *his* family. The devil showed Jesus everything his father used to own—kingdoms that he, the devil, had in his hand. "Look at all the kingdoms of your family here, Jesus. They've been given to me, and I can hand over dominion of them to whomever I choose."

The power of this temptation was that the devil knew Jesus had come for the kingdom. His offer was this: "I'll give it to you if you will just bow down and worship me."

See, it's not a temptation if you don't want it in the first place. It'd be like being offered a chronic case of athlete's foot. All you have to do to get it is say: "Greg, you're great."

"Um...no thanks. I think you're OK, but I don't want any more itchy feet. Thanks just the same."

On the other hand, if the offer was a Ford F-250 with custom pipes, fuzzy dice and a 2" lift kit, I might get a few more compliments tossed my way.

If Jesus had come to restore a religion, the devil would have shown him the world's synagogues, the Shinto shrines, the druids worshiping trees, the reformed druids worshiping bushes. He would have tempted Jesus with the world's religions and the people seeking supernatural power through them. But...he didn't do that. He offered Jesus what the Father had sent him to obtain. "And oh, by the way, you don't have to hang on a cross to get it. Just...bend a knee. See?"

Jesus said "Nope." I'd like to think he answered with something stronger; and wouldn't it have been fitting? Still, Jesus was having none of the devil's offer.

Jesus answered him, "It is written, 'You shall worship the Lord your God and serve Him only.'"

Luke 4:8

"It is written..." What a great phrase! Why? Because it is a legal phrase. God's word is law. Jesus answered with kingdom language—the language of law and culture. He was saying, "In my kingdom, I only worship my Father. That is the only one who gets worshiped in my kingdom. That's the government I come from: God gets the glory; we get to share in his glory."

Satan knew Jesus wanted those kingdoms. It was his best bargaining chip. The devil was willing to give those kingdoms to Jesus to get what he wanted. Adam gave them away to Satan in the garden. Satan now had them as a negotiating piece on this high place of temptation with Jesus. "I'll give you everything your family lost if you worship me."

Worship, in the Greek, means "to kiss, to kiss the ring." Now, you only kiss the ring of a king, and only if you want to show honor and allegiance to that king. Jesus might as well have replied "Kiss this, Satan!" But he was the Son of God, and so, he wisely used scripture.

Why did Satan do that? Well, remember Satan's bucket list? What was on it? His number one goal in life was to exalt his throne above God's throne (ref. Isaiah 14:13). In this passage, we see him trying to do this very thing. "Look, I know you have come after these kingdoms, and I will give them to you, if you'll just worship me."

There are many lessons here. First, don't go to high places with the devil; you might not come down in one piece. Second, we must be careful how we go after that for which God sent us. If we get it illegitimately, we will wind up losing everything. As we grow, we learn about our calling, our purpose. We discover these through our desires. God reveals our purpose through the things that matter to us. Indeed, the yearning qualifies us to receive, for it's the drive that enables us to endure the qualification process.

So, you want to minister to the poor, but you've got to learn how to manage a foodbank. You have to learn accounting, food safety, government regulations, soliciting donations. You have to learn integrity to be trusted with donations. Your ability must grow into your vision. Until it does, you're not ready. Now, if in the meantime, a benefactor comes along and says: "Here, I'll write you a check tomorrow if you stock your warehouses with Acme Markets foodstuffs," it might be what you want, but is it God? Only the Father knows when we are ready. Between wanting and having, there lies a process called qualifying. The devil was offering Jesus a shortcut, and he had an ulterior motive that went way beyond Acme Markets.

Throughout our lives as sons and daughters of God, he will develop us to receive the things he has for us, both to do and to enjoy. But we can't get them the way the world gets them; we can't accept them from the hand of the enemy. The devil's offers abound.

Want to raise an obedient child? *Smack the crap outta him.*

Want a husband? *Put on this skirt and head to the bar.*

Want a better job? *Lie on your resume.*

Want a prestigious title? *Change your business card.*

Want to be like God? *There's this tree in the Garden....*

Our desires are usually not the problem. Most people want things that align with God's goodness. Even sinners want those things. Most people are not intentional doers of evil. Rather, they are misaligned with God's ways and means. Satan is a master at taking our ardent desires as human beings and corrupting us through his proffered solutions. A lie here, a compromise there. "Fake it 'till you make it."

Family Business

Contrary to popular thought, the end does not justify the means; it's the means that kills us. Misaligned, we aim for a worthy goal but do not survive the process.

> Contrary to popular thought, the end doesn't justify the means; in fact, it's the means that often kills us.

The devil offers us our heart's desire in another venue, in another way. He has to. Remember: if we didn't want it, it wouldn't be a temptation. Wanting is not the problem. Ask King David.

Delight yourself in the Lord;
And He will give you the desires of your heart.

Psalm 37:4

The true walk of peace is to receive what God wants us to have, the *way* God wants us to have it. If Jesus would have bowed to temptation, Satan's throne would have been exalted above God's throne. Why? Because Jesus is the Son of God, not just the son of man. The devil would have let Jesus have the kingdoms, but they would have been worthless in God's kingdom because they would have still been in Satan's kingdom, and Satan would have had Jesus in his clutches.

The stakes couldn't have been higher. It wasn't about synagogues, Judaism, old or new religions. It was about government and order, *kosmos*. In this context, it was about Jesus' family kingdom in the world.

Christianity is not about pursuing religion. We are not about being better people. We are about pursuing our Father. It is he who makes us better persons. We don't need messages from popular televangelists: "Seven Ways to Be as Cool as Me!" We don't need self-help programs. We are kingdom people. We are heirs with Jesus. The Kingdom of God changes things. We view the world differently. We are governmental people. We are kings and queens.

Jesus not only rejected the devil's offer, but he rejected his means as well.

> *Jesus replied to him, "It is written: 'YOU SHALL WORSHIP THE LORD YOUR GOD AND SERVE HIM ONLY.'"*
>
> Luke 4:8

Paraphrased, Jesus was saying: "My kingdom has rules. I won't break them. My kingdom, my government, is one of laws and order."

When a Roman boy was adopted, his father made him a partner in the family business. He gave him a ring, a robe and sandals. It was the same with the prodigal son. We are tied to our heavenly Father through our identity, and that carries its own laws.

THE CULTURE OF TRANSFORMATION

Contrary to popular thought, Christians are not sinners saved by grace. We *were* sinners, but now we have been saved by grace. As sons and daughters of the kingdom, our focus is not on sins. Rather, it is on transformation—becoming who God created us to be. Religion wants us to live focused on our sin and failures, but in the kingdom, our focus is on being a son or daughter. Our celebration is about coming out of that sin—that treasonous act—and returning to the Father's house. We rejoice that we are no longer stuck struggling with sin, but instead have been repositioned in God to do the works Jesus did. The question is: do we believe this? No...I mean: do we *really* believe it? How much do we believe this? Belief comes in degrees, doesn't it?

> *Truly, truly, I say to you, he who believes in Me, the works that I do, he will do also; and greater works than these he will do; because I go to the Father. Whatever you ask in My name, that will I do, so that the Father may be glorified in the Son. If you ask Me anything in My name, I will do it.*
>
> John 14:12-14
>
> *Behold, I have given you authority to walk on snakes and scorpions, and authority over all the power of the enemy, and nothing will injure you.*
>
> Luke 10:19

Religion has interpreted "greater works than these" to mean leading people to Jesus and saving them from eternity in hell. The reasoning is this: Jesus never evangelized, so that is our greater work. Well, that sounds plausible, except that is not what these scriptures mean. In Luke 10, Jesus gave us authority. The word *authority* is the word *exousia*, which is another word for "power to act, authority."

God, through Jesus, gave us governmental power to trample on the heads of serpents, scorpions, and all the powers of the enemy. He gave us *dunamis* power, miracle-working power. Amen! We have power to reach into the supernatural realm and pull things into the natural realm. "God, who gives life to the dead and calls into being things that do not exist (Romans 4:17)."

There are things right now that God wants us to have, things that are in the unseen realm. He wants them to manifest in the seen realm. How do we do that? Through kingdom authority, kingdom power and kingdom creativity.

In his letter to the Ephesians, Paul talks about God's power:

And what is the boundless greatness of His power toward us who believe. These are in accordance with the working of the strength of His might.

Ephesians 1:19

Far above all rule and authority and power and dominion, and every name that is named, not only in this age but also in the one to come.

Ephesians 1:21

There's another word for *power*, however: the word *intergeo*, which means, "creative power." God gives us creative power through Holy Spirit. We have God's creative power in our lives. The same spirit that raised Jesus from the dead lives in us. The same things that God did, we can do, because we are made in his image. Now, we are not creating new worlds, but I have seen things created in people's bodies that were not there before we prayed. God can create new limbs, new hearts, new lungs. I've seen him create new eyes. He can do those things where there was no sight. Sight can come, just as it did in Jesus' day. "Jesus Christ is the same yesterday and today and forever" (Hebrews 13:8). He doesn't change. We must change. Religion must change to Kingdom. Religion has removed the power of God from our lives by saying it is no longer available. In fact, it is abundantly available to us, to everyone...when we step into the power of our true identity as sons and daughters of God.

Let's stop living like orphans, immature ones. Let's live like sons and daughters of the King. Jesus was a son. He knew his Father. He knew the things that his Father could manifest through him, and he functioned that way. Religion is dangerous because it strips us of our identity and with it, our power to withstand the enemy.

> *Because you are sons, God has sent forth the Spirit of His Son into our hearts, crying, "Abba! Father!" Therefore you are no longer a slave, but a son; and if a son, then an heir through God.*
>
> Galatians 4:6-7

We are sons and daughters, mature ones, heirs through God. Our inheritance is no longer in our future; it's in our account under our names. It has been released to us! Available now.

Inheritance in Western culture means somebody's got to die for us to get it. (Where there's a will, there's a dead person.) However, in Greco-Roman culture, a son could ask for his inheritance before the father died. This was intended to give the young man the ability to start his life or to expand his father's business. He would take a portion of his father's wealth, the inheritance, and hopefully invest it wisely. The prodigal son is the exception. "Give me mine. I'm outta here!" A child should never have access to her inheritance.

> *However at that time, when you did not know God, you were slaves to those which by nature are not gods.*
>
> Galatians 4:8

Yes, children live in the domain of the kingdom, but they are immature—their thinking is wrong; their mindset is wrong; their handling of things is wrong; their ideology is wrong. Actually, they are barely right about anything. Even the way they relate to the Father is wrong. A child does not know the Father. She knows the things of the Father: comfort, correction, security, provision, but she doesn't know the inner workings of the Father's mind and heart. She won't understand the Father until she matures.

This is why God tells us: "at *that* time when you did not know God." The word *know* is *odiya*, and it means "to perceive." As a child, we are not able to perceive him, to understand him. "You did not know God…" because we "were slaves to those things which by nature are *not* gods." We were being pulled by things we didn't understand, things claiming to be God yet were taking the place of God and ruining our perception of the true God.

Paul identifies the high mark of maturity, even as he admonishes the Galatians.

> *But now that you have come to know God, or rather to be known by God, how is it that you turn back again to the weak and worthless elemental things, to which you desire to be enslaved all over again?*
>
> Galatians 4:9

"But now that you have come to know God, or rather to be known by God…." Now you might be thinking: *I thought God knew me already. I thought when I was born again that God knew me.* Yes, God knows you just like we know our children. But that is not what it means. It doesn't mean "to become acquainted with." It's deeper. It means that God has looked at us, examined us, and determined: "Now I can trust you. You can partner with me in the family business. I know you because I know that you know me. You know the way I act, the way I talk, the way I represent myself to people. You know the way that I want things done, and I know how you do things.

In the Old Testament, God made a similar appraisal of Abraham—the patriarch of the Jewish nation. After telling him to sacrifice his son,

Isaac, he yelled "Stop," as the knife made its deadly arc. Then God said something profound.

> *"Do not lay a hand on the boy," he said. "Do not do anything to him. Now I know that you fear God, because you have not withheld from me your son, your only son."*
>
> Genesis 22:12 NIV

That is an awesome phrase: "Now I know..." God learned something about Abraham in that moment, something he did not know a moment before. Paul said it this way:

> *For now we see only a reflection as in a mirror; then we shall see face to face. Now I know in part; then I shall know fully, even as I am fully known.*
>
> 1 Corinthians 13:12

"I shall know fully, even as I am fully known." Make sense? We get to know the Father as he gets to know us. It is from this mutual knowing that the strength of the relationship is realized.

How We See God

As a good Baptist boy (as if there is any other kind), I was raised to believe that once I was saved, I was always saved. Now, we need to understand that the word *saved*, as used by this religion, meant a ticket to heaven. But one of my pastors also told me that before I go to bed every night, I needed to say my prayers to confess all my sins. Why? Because if I died in my sins, I'd go to hell. No wonder I was crazy! This was schizophrenic Christianity. *You are saved, always saved, but...pray to not go to hell.* Fear was the defining quality of my relationship with this being called God. It's as if Jesus taught his disciples to pray: "Our Father, who is in heaven, thank you for saving us for eternity, and oh by the way, please don't cast us into hell." (Jesus might have lost a disciple or two over that one.)

Religion—especially the religion we've been raised in—hinders many in the world today from pursuing Jesus. The proverb says:

Family Business

Train up a child in the way he should go,
Even when he grows older he will not abandon it.

Proverbs 22:6

Of course, we read this scripture through the lens of earnest Christian parents: *Here's how to raise godly kids.* But that's not what it says. This proverb identifies a principle that works regardless of what the child is trained in. Ever notice that children of Muslims grow up to be Muslims? Baptist children become Baptist. Eskimo children become Eskimos and learn 99 words for "snow." This is because the early years of a child's life are the prime years for training. Yes, many of us diverge from our childhood training, but it will always be a part of us. (People tell me I still preach with a Baptist preacher's cadence.) This proverb identifies the daunting task we have of changing an entire generation that has not been raised with an appreciation for God. Change is not always pretty. Modern Germany is often praised as the model country for order, prosperity and security. Indeed, it runs like clockwork and its citizens are mostly happy, but it took a world war to afford the population a clean start.

We currently have an entire generation of young people who refuse to attend a church service. They see Christianity as powerless, full of hypocrites and offering conflicting messages of salvation, mercy and eternal damnation. Fundamentally, they see a lack of love in its adherents. This opens the door for deception. A deceiver doesn't have to be completely right about something to sway popular opinion. Deception only has to be more right than the example laid out before an audience. When the example is abysmal, the pickings are easy.

Today's generation rejects rules and regulations because they seem constricting. They understand the Christian life as a struggle to live perfectly and to give their lives to some undefined being who dwells somewhere in the universe. This is bundled with the hope of spending eternity with this being that they don't have a prayer of ever knowing. *There is no way to relate to him; he's just out there and he's beyond me, so he must be holy (because I certainly am not).*

When we are raised to think of God as both holy and remote, we tend to see ourselves as fundamentally unclean. Why else has God removed himself? (As religion erroneously teaches.) Indeed, we easily imagine ourselves as the epicenter of all that is evil in the world. Hence, the farther from ourselves something appears, the holier it becomes in our minds. Said another way: to remain good, God must stay far away, for we are so evil.

Such faulty logic is endemic in society today; it is matched only by the rising numbers of depressed, anxious and suicidal people. We have given this generation a religion—secular humanism is a religion—that has skewed their identity and prevented them from knowing the true Father.

How do we fix this mess?

For starters, we must repent. We must change how we think about religion, and we must change how we relate to religion. Getting rid of religion is a start, but it's not the complete solution. Otherwise, we'll lose the baby with the bath water. Religion cannot be cast out of society. Religion represents something real...even though it distorts the real. We must displace religion with something better: kingdom.

Casting out a spirit of religion is also not the answer. The spirit of religion is not your everyday little demon. It is a strong man—a principality—and it will more than likely be here until the Lord returns.

We displace the ideas spawned by the spirit of religion, and we replace them with ideas deposited by Holy Spirit. In so doing, we remove religion's ability to guide our thoughts. We don't allow it to control our identity. Every time something religious comes up in our lives, we ask the Father: "What does kingdom look like in this situation?" And we let him teach us.

That will change everything. It will change the way we do church. We are not supposed to be *doing* church or *going* to church. Did Jesus ever tell us to *go to* church? No. He told us *we are* the church. Church is not an event. Church is not cathedrals. It's not steeples or stained-glass windows. Sure, we've written songs about them. We call it *church*. We have taken the biblical definition of church and redefined it to be buildings, an event or an experience when Jesus never intended for it to be any of these things.

> *And I also say to you that you are Peter, and upon this rock I will build My church; and the gates of Hades will not overpower it.*
>
> Matthew 16:18

Recall our four questions:

- Who is speaking?
- Who are they speaking to?
- What does it mean in their culture?
- How do we apply it to our lives?

With this line of inquiry, when we read the word *church*, what does it mean? It means we are the *ekklesia*, the legislative arm of God in the earth. Church is part of our identity; it is who we are—a part of our kingdom DNA. That is church.

Now, we can enter a building where the church gathers, or we can go downtown to the roughest bar in town. Either place, we would still be in church. Church is not brick and mortar. Church is flesh and blood...and spirit! It is who we are. Everywhere we go, there is church. We carry the legislative arm of God, the power of the government, the *kosmos* of heaven.

This is how change happens. If we find ourselves doing something differently than how Jesus intended, we must be willing to reevaluate. We need to walk our religion into an interrogation room and have at it. We need to know *why* we believe what we believe. How well is what we are doing pleasing to God? If what we believe turns out to be unbiblical, we must repent, get it out of our lives, and receive what belongs in its place.

Certainly, this will upset many people. Good. They need to be upset. Many cannot accept church as a governmental body instead of a religious experience. That's fine. Those of us who can, need to think.

We need to evaluate what we are doing. For too long, we have blamed the ineffectiveness of the church on the devil when something else is hindering us from being who God created us to be. In fact, it looks a lot like us.

Unshakable

See to it that you do not refuse Him who is speaking. For if those did not escape when they refused him who warned them on earth, much less will we escape who turn away from Him who warns from heaven. And His voice shook the earth then, but now He has promised, saying, "YET ONCE MORE I WILL SHAKE NOT ONLY THE EARTH, BUT ALSO THE HEAVEN." This expression, "Yet once more," denotes the removing of those things which can be shaken, as of created things, so that those things which cannot be shaken may remain. Therefore, since you receive a kingdom which cannot be shaken, let us show gratitude, by which we may offer to God an acceptable service with reverence and awe; for our God is a consuming fire.

Hebrews 12:25-29

This is quite a promise: everything that can be shaken will be shaken. Yet God has given us a kingdom that cannot be shaken—a kingdom, not a religion, not a theology, not an eschatology, but a king's domain that will endure forever. *God, shift us out of our religious traditions.*

Jesus told the Pharisees that traditions have caused the word of God to not work.

> *[You] thereby invalidating the word of God by your tradition which you have handed down; and you do many things such as that.*

Mark 7:13

Family Business

If God does not change—if he's the same as he's always been—then why don't the blind see, the deaf hear and the lame walk? Why are the dead not raised more often? Why aren't people hungry for God and forcing their way into the Kingdom of God? It is because of the power of religion. Religion is our greatest adversary.

> The Kingdom of God is here, and it is coming in a greater way. It is in us; it is in everyone who is born again. The authority and power of God are available now!

The good news is that the Kingdom of God cannot be shaken. The Kingdom of God is here, and it is coming in a greater way. It is in us; it is in everyone who is born again. The authority and power of God are available now! We can face our tomorrow, to be who God created us to be, carrying governmental order with us. Religion tells us to throw lifelines to rescue the lost into heaven. Jesus never said to throw a lifeline. He said to bring government rule and break the darkness off of their lives, then escort them back home.

There are two great commissions in the Bible: Matthew 28 is about discipling nations.

> *And Jesus came up and spoke to them, saying, "All authority in heaven and on earth has been given to Me. Go, therefore, and make disciples of all the nations, baptizing them in the name of the Father and the Son and the Holy Spirit, teaching them to follow all that I commanded you; and behold, I am with you always, to the end of the age."*
>
> Matthew 28:18-20

Mark 16 is about getting the family back, bringing people back. It is our responsibility to bring people out of darkness and back into the power of their true identity.

> *And He said to them, "Go into all the world and preach the gospel to all creation. The one who has believed and has been baptized will be saved; but the one who has not*

believed will be condemned. These signs will accompany those who have believed: in My name they will cast out demons, they will speak with new tongues; they will pick up serpents, and if they drink any deadly poison, it will not harm them; they will lay hands on the sick, and they will recover."

Mark 16:15-18

Our responsibility as sons and daughters of the kingdom is to walk in governmental authority, not in religious experience. When we face the enemy, we are facing things contrary to the kingdom culture God has given us: healing, health, wholeness, joy, peace, fruits of the Spirit, gifts of the Spirit. We don't have to feel anointed. We don't have to look anointed. We *are* anointed by inherent rights as sons and daughters of the King. Our power is not of feelings; that's religion—an event of feeling. Our power is of identity. Kingdom is an event of authority; it is a lifestyle of authority.

Let us be firm in our identity. Shake off the religious mindset that says we are weak, worthless, unworthy, barely making it. Break this off in the name of Jesus. We are sons and daughters of the King. We are worth everything Jesus paid to purchase us back into the family. We are worth his life. It is our privilege to partner with him in bringing heaven to earth.

What is heaven on earth? It is the will and intent of God's heart manifesting where we are. Amen!

4

Dominion of the King

AS SONS AND DAUGHTERS OF THE KING, we are called to life; we are called to be the light of mankind.

> *In the beginning was the Word, and the Word was with God, and the Word was God. He was in the beginning with God. All things came into being through Him, and apart from Him not even one thing came into being that has come into being. In Him was life, and the life was the Light of mankind. And the Light shines in the darkness, and the darkness did not grasp it.*
>
> John 1:1-5

Wherever we are: at home, work, school, or rushing between all three, we must realize that God never called us to make a living. That is not our focus. He called us to bring life.

God will take care of our living. In a kingdom, the King is responsible for its citizens. (Note: we are citizens, not subjects.) The assurance that we are cared for lifts a burden from our lives as we go about our day. We are more than people trying to survive in life. We are missionaries. We are God's ambassadors to the sphere of influence in which we are engaged. Our mission field is not necessarily somewhere overseas but everywhere we place our foot.

> *Every place that the sole of your foot will tread upon I have given to you, as I promised to Moses.*
>
> Joshua 1:3

Like any missionary, we face obstacles; indeed, there are enemies trying to hinder us from doing what God has called us to do. But as sons and daughters of God, we have the upper hand. Paul faced adversaries continually in his ministry; they impeded him, but they did not stop him.

> *But I will remain in Ephesus until Pentecost; for a wide door for effective service has opened to me, and there are many adversaries.*
>
> 1 Corinthians 16:8-9

Paul had a call on his life. A door was open to his ministry, but there were also many enemies seeking to rush through that door. We face this today. There are enemies at the gates of our lives, but there is also victory.

> *We are from God, little children, and have overcome them; because greater is He who is in you than he who is in the world.*
>
> 1 John 4:4

> *So shall they fear*
> *The name of the Lord from the west,*
> *And His glory from the rising of the sun;*
> *When the enemy comes in like a flood,*
> *The Spirit of the Lord will lift up a standard against him.*
>
> Isaiah 59:19 NKJV

Wherever we go, living out our assignment as sons and daughters, we are on the mission field. We live out our purpose. We are intentional about our destiny. The assignment of our life is not to hang out till Jesus comes, but to shift people out of the Kingdom of Darkness into the Kingdom of Light.

How do we do that? We live in our identity. We learn to be very comfortable in our skin.

So many Christians are intimidated by being in the world. Yet scripture says that part of our assignment is to cause the kingdoms of this world to become the kingdom of our Christ.

> *Then the seventh angel sounded; and there were loud voices in heaven, saying, "The kingdom of the world has become the kingdom of our Lord and of His Christ; and He will reign forever and ever."*
>
> Revelation 11:15

That will not happen unless we engage the world; engage the system; not succumbing to it but engaging it. We are in this world, but we are not of the world.

> *I [Jesus] am not asking You [the Father] to take them out of the world, but to keep them away from the evil one. They are not of the world, just as I am not of the world. Sanctify them in the truth; Your word is truth.*
>
> John 17:15-17

Remember, *world* means, "governmental structures or governmental order." It doesn't mean "a sinful atmosphere," even though a sinful atmosphere exists. The Greek word is *kosmos*, and it refers to a governmental structure and order. That is an important distinction.

When we read *this world* with our religious minds and Western culture, we think of darkness, sin and all kinds of evil—all the things we are supposed to avoid. But Jesus never told us to be removed from the world. He expected us to get into the world as change agents. We don't let the world affect us; we affect the world! The world doesn't shape us; we shape the world.

Remember, the earth and the world are two different things. The Bible says:

> *The earth is the Lord's, and all it contains,*
> *The world, and those who live in it.*
>
> Psalm 24:1

God never lost the earth. He lost the world. The word *world* is "governed, governmental structure." That could also be the word *kingdom*. And the Kingdom of God is available to us today. The Kingdom of God *has come*, and the Kingdom of God *will come*. It doesn't mean the Kingdom of God is not here. The word *kingdom* is made up of two words: *king* and *dominion*. So, when we are talking about *kingdom*, we are talking about "the dominion of the King."

We are not referring to this false doctrine called Dominion Theology. It was the idea that we were going to make everything in the world perfect and present it to Jesus. Well, it isn't going to be that way. The world will get better, but not without God's involvement and our partnership.

> *"You are the light of the world. A city set on a hill cannot be hidden; nor do people light a lamp and put it under a basket, but on the lampstand, and it gives light to all who are in the house. Your light must shine before people in such a way that they may see your good works, and glorify your Father who is in heaven.*
>
> Matthew 5:14-16

Each time light enters darkness, darkness flees. The only way the world will get worse is if we withdraw our light. So, let your light shine, for light dispels darkness. The world that God has given us is getting brighter because we are in it. Don't believe the news media; believe the word of God.

Religion says we must tolerate darkness. Kingdom says different. Yes, there will be darkness, but we "are the light of the world." We are the light of the *kosmos*—the governmental structures and rule that is in the earth.

When God sets a son or daughter in the midst of a dark place, light dispels the darkness. When we step into that place, heaven steps in with us. We are not alone. Did God not say he will not desert us or abandon us?

Be strong and courageous, do not be afraid or in dread of them, for the Lord your God is the One who is going with you. He will not desert you or abandon you.

And the Lord is the one who is going ahead of you; He will be with you. He will not desert you or abandon you. Do not fear and do not be dismayed."

Deuteronomy 31:6 & 8

He said it, and he meant it. We can take God at his word.

God is not a man, that He would lie,
Nor a son of man, that He would change His mind;
Has He said, and will He not do it?
Or has He spoken, and will He not make it good?

Numbers 23:19

People might let you down. They promise to never leave you nor forsake you, and then they file for divorce. They pledge their undying support and next thing you know, they run off to somewhere else. Guess what? People fail. They lie. They're far from perfect. Jesus knew this well.

Now when He was in Jerusalem at the Passover, during the feast, many believed in His name as they observed His signs which He was doing. But Jesus, on His part, was not entrusting Himself to them, because He knew all people, and because He did not need anyone to testify about mankind, for He Himself knew what was in mankind.

John 2:23-25

Jesus knew what was in mankind. Here's the good news. God is perfect. He will not divorce us. He will not leave us.

Fear not, for you will not be put to shame;
And do not feel humiliated, for you will not be disgraced;
But you will forget the shame of your youth,
And no longer remember the disgrace of your widowhood.
For your husband is your Maker,

> *Whose name is the Lord of armies;*
> *And your Redeemer is the Holy One of Israel,*
> *Who is called the God of all the earth.*
> *For the Lord has called you,*
> *Like a wife forsaken and grieved in spirit,*
> *Even like a wife of one's youth when she is rejected.*
>
> Isaiah 54:4-6

When we give our lives to God, he will not walk out of our lives. He will engage our lives. He has a purpose for us. "Let's go take back the world!"

A New World Order

God is not mad at the world. He is not mad at the governmental structures or order. When the enemy took it from Adam, it became disorder. He is not mad about that. God does not want to destroy the earth. He is going to remake it. When he returns and we are caught up to meet him in the air, he will remake the earth. There will be a new heaven and a new earth.

> *Then I saw a new heaven and a new earth; for the first heaven and the first earth passed away, and there is no longer any sea. And I saw the holy city, new Jerusalem, coming down out of heaven from God, prepared as a bride adorned for her husband.*
>
> Revelation 21:1-2

There will also be a new order, a new governmental structure, a new world set in the earth. In the earth, there are many worlds. There are many *kosmos*, many governmental structures and rules. Jesus did not come to destroy them. He came to get them back, to take the world back. He already owned the earth, but he came to take the world back with their governmental structures.

God owns the world by inherent right. The enemy stepped in and took the structure that God set in place to govern His earth. Think of a landlord renting property. If the renters don't do right, they are evicted. God has already evicted folks from his property called earth when he flooded the world. Wickedness had become so bad that he issued the eviction notice, saying, "A hard rain's a gonna fall." Then he started over with a righteous man named Noah.

God owns the earth; he owns everything in it. He is a God of order and process. He does things legally according to governmental structure. He is taking back the kingdoms of the world. He is taking back the order, the rule and the structure of the *kosmos* through you and through me—his ekklesia. Jesus, through the great commission of Matthew 28, sends us into all the world to teach them to observe everything he has taught us.

> *And Jesus came up and spoke to them, saying, "All authority has been given to Me in heaven and on earth. Go therefore and make disciples of all the nations, baptizing them in the name of the Father and the Son and the Holy Spirit, teaching them to observe all that I commanded you; and lo, I am with you always, even to the end of the age."*
>
> Matthew 28:18-20

BORN AGAIN

Now let's look at John 3 and one of the most famous verses in the Bible.

> *Now there was a man of the Pharisees, named Nicodemus, a ruler of the Jews; this man came to Jesus by night and said to Him, "Rabbi, we know that You have come from God as a teacher; for no one can do these signs that You do unless God is with him." Jesus answered and said to him, "Truly, truly, I say to you, unless one is born again he cannot see the kingdom of God.*
>
> *Nicodemus said to Him, "How can a person be born when he is old? He cannot enter his mother's womb a second time and be born, can he?" Jesus answered, "Truly, truly, I say to*

> *you, unless someone is born of water and the Spirit, he cannot enter the kingdom of God."*
>
> John 3:1-5

Nicodemus was "a man of the Pharisees...." Pharisees were religious men. Clearly, he was bound by religion. When we see Pharisees, we see religion. They were religion on steroids. These were the people whom Jesus accused of making his Father's house a den of thieves.

> *And Jesus entered the temple area and drove out all those who were selling and buying on the temple grounds, and He overturned the tables of the money changers and the seats of those who were selling doves. And He said to them, "It is written: 'My house will be called a house of prayer'; but you are making it a den of robbers."*
>
> Matthew 21-12-13

> Clearly, Jesus was not interested in partnering with religion, and certainly not with the Jewish religion or the system that God gave them through Moses.

By their fruit, we shall know them. If the Pharisees were right with God, they wouldn't have allowed those tables to be installed. Jesus called them hypocrites, children of hell, and whitewashed tombs. I don't think Jesus liked them very much.

Now, remember when we study scripture, we need to know who is talking and who they are talking to. We cannot interpret it through a Western lens. We have to understand what it meant in that culture and then figure out how to apply it in our lives. Maybe we don't want to invade the nearest denominational church and turn over their tables—it's probably a Sunday School bake sale anyway—but we can have some other positive impact.

Clearly, Jesus was not interested in partnering with religion, and certainly not with the Jewish religion or the system that God gave them through Moses. Over the centuries, they corrupted it, taking it far from what God intended. God, through Jesus, was not interested in redeeming the Jewish religion. He was, however, interested in redeeming the Jewish people. God is not against the Jewish people. We are one new man. If they are born again and we are born again, then we are one new man, but Jewish people have to be born again.

There's a popular theology that says Jewish people get a pass to heaven. Well, they don't. They must be born again like everyone else. How do I know? Because of what Nicodemus said to Jesus in John 3: "Rabbi, we know that you have come from God as a teacher; for no one can do these signs that you do unless God is with him."

This is a powerful testimony from a leader of a religious order opposed to Jesus. They knew who Jesus was and where he came from. Of course, they did! If they had judged him a fake, would they have fought so hard to stop him?

Jesus answered: "Unless one is born again he cannot see the kingdom of God." He did not say, "Unless one is born again, he cannot enter into my new religion." The Kingdom of God is a governmental structure. This king's dominion has absolutely zero to do with religion. This is what we are unseating and displacing out of our lives.

Nicodemus was befuddled: "How can a man be born again when he is old? He cannot enter the second time into his mother's womb and be born, can he?"

Jesus answered, "Unless someone is born of water and the Spirit, he cannot enter the kingdom of God." Not a religion, but a kingdom. The Kingdom of God is a nation, a country. A religion also has territory. It's a rectangular box about 7 feet by 3 feet and it goes in the ground.

> *That which is born of the flesh is flesh, and that which is born of the Spirit is spirit. Do not be amazed that I said to you, 'You must be born again.' The wind blows where it wishes and you hear the sound of it, but do not know where it comes from and where it is going; so is everyone who is born of the Spirit."*
>
> John 3:6-8

And Jesus continued his conversation with the Pharisee:

Nicodemus said to Him, "How can these things be?"

Jesus answered and said to him, "Are you the teacher of Israel and do not understand these things? Truly, truly, I say to you, we speak of what we know and testify of what we have seen, and you do not accept our testimony. If I told you earthly things and you do not believe, how will you believe if I tell you heavenly things? No one has ascended into heaven, but He who descended from heaven: the Son of Man. As Moses lifted up the serpent in the wilderness, even so must the Son of Man be lifted up; so that whoever believes will in Him have eternal life."

John 3:9-15

Herein lies the answer to the fundamental question: Why did God send his son?

For God so loved the world, that He gave His only begotten Son, that whoever believes in Him shall not perish, but have eternal life.

John 3:16

God loved the world. It was worth the life of his son to him. With the arrival of Jesus, the Kingdom of God invaded the earthly realm and the supernatural realm, the seen and the unseen. God loved the *kosmos*. He loved the governmental structure, authority, rule. He loved order. For God so loved the *kosmos*, the world. This word *world* has nothing to do with humanity; nothing to do with you or me. It has to do with positioning, that which God created us to do. So, we can read John 3:16 this way: "For God so loved order, governmental structure and authority that he sent his only begotten Son into the corrupt governmental structure, that whosoever believes in him should not perish, but live eternally with God."

For God did not send His Son into the world to condemn the world, but that the world through Him might be saved.

John 3:17

Dominion of the King

God did not send Jesus to condemn or judge the world. Jesus was not sent into the *kosmos*, the governmental structure, the order or the disorder, to condemn it or to destroy it. Rather, that the world might be saved through him.

Now, this word *saved* comes from the root word *so* in the Greek, which is why Nicodemus replied: "*So* what?" Today, under the influence of religion, we think *saved* means getting our ticket to heaven; we've bought our fire insurance; we're not going to hell.

Well, being saved does mean we're going to heaven, but that's not all it means. Yes, when we die in the Lord, we go to heaven. Paul said to be absent from the body is to be present with the Lord (ref. 2 Corinthians 5:8). But this word *saved* is deeper than just something that we will have eternally. Being saved—being born again with the assurance of living eternally as sons and daughters—does not mean eternity starts when we die. Eternity starts when we are born again.

If we are saved, we have already entered into eternity. We will never die. Yes, our flesh will fall dead one day, and we'll have a funeral, and nice people will say nice things about how much they liked us and didn't he write nice books. Then they'll drop our corpse into the ground, toss in some dirt, and rush home to catch the Ole Miss game.

But there is so much more to being *saved* than simply going to heaven. The word *saved* means "cured, to restore." We could divide that to "re-store" and there the "re" stem in front of a word means "to do it again, to recover, to make well, to preserve."

Here's an example of saved. Let's say I was the creator of the Little Yapper Dog Jacket. This is my idea, my dream, my vision. I hold the patent for a jacket to keep little yapper dogs warm in winter. Nobody else thought about it. (Of course, they didn't.) Well, I create the jacket and put it on my dog. The jacket is now living in its purpose. I have "stored" it there. I placed it there to do what I created it to do—keep the little yapper dog outside so I can get some peace.

One dark winter day, the jacket falls off the dog and is trampled in the snow. The jacket is now removed from the place that it was originally intended to function. *Oh no!* Visions of little yapper dogs lying frozen all over the earth, their little legs sticking up in the air! So, I say, "I'm going to save this jacket. It has value; it has purpose. I'm going to "restore" it. So, I dig it out of the snow and put in on the cat. (She's not happy about it.)

Now, have I restored the jacket? No, I have not. Well, it's back on an animal. Doesn't that mean it's restored? No. It was not created to cover the cat. It was created to cover this insufferable maniac of narcissistic frenzy. So, the jacket is never restored until I put it back in the same place that I originally intended for it to function—the shivering little yapper dog.

Religion says we can't be restored like that. Religion says we have to die and go to heaven before we can be in that spot. But Jesus said to Nicodemus that the world will be restored, recovered and saved— put back into God's original intent for his design. That is empowering, even for yapper dogs.

Jesus said, "the one who believes in Me, the works that I do, he will do also; and greater works than these he will do; because I am going to the Father" (John 14:12). Religion disqualifies us from that promise with false images of our supposed inadequacies. Consider Paul's dissertation on God's gifts to the church:

> But to each one of us grace was given according to the measure of Christ's gift. Therefore He says:
>
> "When He ascended on high, He led captivity captive, and gave gifts to men."
>
> (Now this, "He ascended"—what does it mean but that He also first descended into the lower parts of the earth? He who descended is also the One who ascended far above all the heavens, that He might fill all things.)
>
> And He Himself gave some to be apostles, some prophets, some evangelists, and some pastors and teachers, for the

equipping of the saints for the work of ministry, for the edifying of the body of Christ, till we all come to the unity of the faith and of the knowledge of the Son of God, to a perfect man, to the measure of the stature of the fullness of Christ; that we should no longer be children, tossed to and fro and carried about with every wind of doctrine, by the trickery of men, in the cunning craftiness of deceitful plotting, but, speaking the truth in love, may grow up in all things into Him who is the head—Christ—from whom the whole body, joined and knit together by what every joint supplies, according to the effective working by which every part does its share, causes growth of the body for the edifying of itself in love.

Ephesians 4:7-16 NKJV

God gave gifts to the church. Why did he give these gifts? Because God is putting us back where he originally intended us to be. Religion tells us we'll never be restored until the Lord returns. Well...that's not in the Bible; it's in Western theology. We've been reading too many books by religious people. We need to read *The Book* and ask: "Who's talking? Who are they talking to? What did it mean in that culture? How do I apply this to my life?"

The five-fold ministry is given to us for the equipping of the saints, for the work of service to the building up of the body of Christ until we attain to the unity of faith. These goals are priorities that God intends the five-fold ministry to do. Five-fold gifts are never called to build their own ministry. They are called to serve the body in doing what God called it to do: "till you all come to the unity of the faith and of the knowledge of the Son of God...."

The next statement destroys this religious idea that we've been talking about. It says, "to a perfect man, to the measure of the stature of the fullness of Christ." Sounds like "restored" to me! Our responsibility as apostles, prophets, pastors, teachers and evangelists is to equip the saints, to bring all of us into that restored place where we become "a perfect man," meaning mature men and women.

"To the measure...." The word *measure* is the Greek word *metron,* and it means "proper standard or proper measurement."

"Of the stature," is translated from the Greek word *hélikia*. It means "maturity, the life of, or the stature of, that which belongs to the fullness." The word *fullness* is the Greek word *pleróma*, and it means the same: "filling up to contain what the other contained, fulfillment, or full, to be amply supplied as another, to be finished as another, and to carry oneself as another, of the fullness of Christ."

Religion says we can't have that. *Well, that is for after the Lord returns, when we are here on this new earth and doing whatever we'll be doing in that time. That's when we'll have that full measure of Christ.*

Folks, the five-fold ministry gifts will not be needed on the new earth. We have no idea through scripture that those gifts will actually be functioning after the return of the Lord. The five-fold ministry gifts are for now.

THEOLOGY AND THE UNKNOWN

We do not study theology to reinforce our present doctrine. We study to question our doctrine. We ask *why*, not because we are full of doubts, but because we understand that this is the progression to true theology—that which reveals truth.

You will know the truth, and the truth will set you free.

John 8:32

We are not promoting something a denomination gave us. It is not something we read out of a book. It is not something that we created to justify our tragic lives. So many times, we rewrite our theologies to fit those areas of life that don't seem to make sense. Let's be real: even the best of lives contain questions, events, even fears for which we have no cogent answer. Paul calls these things mysteries, and they are vital to our growth. Why? Because only by admitting what you don't know can you press into greater learning. Who enrolls into school when they feel they have nothing to learn? It's the hungry mind, the yearning heart, the aching spirit that cries out for answers and is filled.

> *Blessed are those who hunger and thirst for righteousness, for they will be satisfied.*
>
> Matthew 5:6

When we accept a contorted theology, one that warps and bends to accommodate our need to have all the answers, we end up living beneath what God intended. God is not afraid of our inquiries. Indeed, he relishes them. Ours is the Father who pleads with us in Isaiah 1:18:

> *"Come now, and let us reason together,"*
> *Says the Lord,*
> *"Though your sins are like scarlet,*
> *They shall be as white as snow;*
> *Though they are red like crimson,*
> *They shall be as wool.*
>
> Isaiah 1:18 NKJV

An invitation to reason with God; to what aim? To realize the priceless gift of the forgiveness of sin. We need to constantly question our theology.

What is theology? It is the way we see God, the things we believe about God, and the way we relate to God. We get our theology from our ideologies and philosophies, and we create a theology to relate to God. Because this is a huge subject, we must ask: to what extent are we relating to God biblically and culturally?

To be a mature one—to grow as sons and daughters as Paul described in Ephesians—we need to understand God's goal for our lives. This requires the five-fold giftings to work together to bring us into this place that God has designed for us. Moving from a place of ignorance (not knowing) to a place of knowledge is called learning. But don't miss the starting point. It is vital. We must question what we believe and face our ignorance to uncover things we don't know. There are so many things we assumed we knew; things we did not realize we were deficient in...until challenged. Do we believe what we say we believe? To what extent do we believe what we believe? Honest questions deserve honest appraisals.

I speak from experience.

THE BARN

When I was 17 years old, still a good Baptist boy, I got an invite to play trumpet in a Charismatic church. A prophet named Leland Davis was ministering. At the time of the altar call, a boy came out of the second row and walked right up on the platform. Leland laid his hands on him, and the boy fell forward. He didn't fall backward. He fell forward and began to speak in tongues. I was stunned. I went to the pastor after church, Pastor Cecil. I didn't know him. It was my first night in this place. And I said, "Brother Cecil, I want what that boy got. Would y'all pray for me?"

To my surprise, he said, "No, we're not going to pray for you tonight. Take this pamphlet, go home and read it."

It was by Pat Robinson on the baptism of the Holy Spirit. I went home and read that thing 100 times. I was the first one at the door the next night, trumpet in hand. I played like Gideon that night, and I couldn't wait for altar call. In my hometown church, we were told if we speak in tongues, it was the devil. But I saw it firsthand and knew deep inside that it was real, that it was God, and I wanted it.

At the altar call, Pastor Cecil announced: "There's some here who want the baptism of the Holy Spirit tonight. Come on up."

I strode to the platform, and before Prophet Leland could touch me, the Spirit of God hit me like 500 volts, and I started speaking in tongues. I experienced something I was taught was wrong, but it was really right. I heard the voice of the Lord that night say: *"Greg, you are going to have to unlearn almost as much as you've learned."*

Now, I'm in the spirit, but I'm battling in my mind: *Whoa, wait a minute. If I abandon those traditions, then I'm dishonoring those who taught me—good people, family members who love me, parishioners who tolerate me, pastors who try their best with me.* But that wasn't true. I saw that God was building on what they taught me. I knew there was a just God because the Baptists taught me that. They also taught me about Jesus, the cross and the resurrection. But I'd reached the limit of what they had to offer. See, inferior theology isn't the death knell of Christianity; it's a hinderance to those of us who want to grow beyond it. Like a pair of pants that I wore in the fourth grade, they no longer fit. I'd grown beyond them. Had I stayed in them, I might never have walked normally again. No, I didn't know what I needed until I saw it, but I knew I needed something. I was hungry, curious, searching, even desperate. I was ready, and I knew it when God showed it to me. He had prepared me.

There are things we cling to for decades, believing this is the way it is. *I was taught this way. Grandma believed it. Great Grandma believed it. Great great grandma probably believed it too, had she stayed sober. So, I'm gonna believe it. Bless God!* He's the same yesterday, today and forever! He never changes, and my beliefs will never change...until they need to change. Either that, or I spend the rest of my life in fourth-grade pants.

If you allow Holy Spirit to bring you to a place of unlearning, he will lead you to a place of great learning. I'm still in that process. God is helping me unlearn old things and learn new things. It's a powerful, awesome journey. Nothing boring or mundane about it. I wake up every morning excited about what Holy Spirit is doing in my life that day...if I will allow him to lead me.

Early in my spiritual growth, I thought of my grandfather, who was a Baptist minister all his life. I feared that if I moved on from the things he taught me, I would be dishonoring him. I didn't want to dishonor my granddaddy. I loved him from a little boy. At eight years old, when I got born again, I clung to his coattails. I went to church with him. Sat on the front row sometimes. When I got into trouble, I had to sit on the platform with him. But God was positioning me. Granddaddy would say: "Greg, stop that! Get up here and sit right here on that step." Kind of an altar call for a precocious prodigy, I suppose.

And I had to listen. There was no such thing as "disobey Granddaddy." No Siree! I believed in eternal life, but I wasn't ready to go at that instant. I followed him everywhere. We went to cow sales. We worked in the barn. We went on crusades. Why? Because of the hunger inside me. I drew from my grandfather, from his essence. He was a minister for more than 75 years. I wanted that in my life. He helped start over 200 churches in America and in several nations for the Baptist organization. That is still in my DNA. I didn't have to unlearn that; that is part of who I am. My Grandfather was an apostle and didn't know it; he didn't have the language for it. But that's who he was and what he did. He had the fruit of it.

The day that I told him, at the age of 17, that I'd received the baptism of the Holy Spirit and I felt called to the ministry, he said, "Greg, if you can do anything else, do it."

He didn't say this because he didn't want me hurt. He didn't care if I got hurt in ministry. He knew that would happen. He was telling me, "Greg, if there's anything else in your heart you can do, do it instead. Don't do this. But if it's all you can do, then do it."

"This is all I can do," I said. "This is what I'm called to do."

"Follow me," he said.

We walked from his house over to the barn. He was wearing these big white mule brand work gloves. I followed him to the tack room where he kept things for the cattle.

"Kneel down, Son."

He took off those big gloves and laid his hands on me. A Baptist guy! They didn't do that stuff, but he did. Laying his hands on me, he prayed over me, blessed me, spoke things over me concerning my ministry and my life. I'll never forget it. For years after, I visited my grandfather's farm and drew from his wisdom. That barn is still standing and I'm still kneeling.[5]

> That barn is still standing and I'm still kneeling.

I've had to unlearn many things. Unlearning is not dishonor; it is honor. That day in the barn, my grandfather knew he wasn't recreating his ministry in me. No, he was extending it through me. We never discussed it much, but I'm sure there were things he didn't know, and he knew he didn't know—things about God, about being a Christian, about why faith worked sometimes and didn't work other times. Being a Baptist for him was about enduring, about soldiering forth. To his credit, he was ready to pass on his spiritual life to the next generation. He couldn't draw a map to the spiritual realms to which I was headed, but he knew they lay beyond him, and in his love—for God and for me—he released me with all he had. Raise a child in the way he is bent…and then let him go. Praise God.

A New Foundation

God builds on the foundations laid before us. Much of the world knows of Jesus from the Baptists. Today, they are learning kingdom from us.

Where is a theology validated? How do we evaluate what we believe? It is through the word of God. The truth of scripture must be understood through the culture in which it was written, not through modern culture, not even through good ole' Southern culture. (Tho I have it on good authority that Jesus said "Y'all." Feel free to argue with Granddaddy if you like.)

So, when Jesus came to the earth, he did so to save God's order and governmental structure. God so loved order that he sent his only begotten Son into disorder so that the disorder may be restored to

---

[5] A photo of that barn is on the back cover of this book.

order. And that everyone who believes in Him will not perish, but have eternal life. That phrase *believes in him* doesn't mean just to say the name of Jesus or pray a certain prayer. From the Greek definition, believe literally means "to buy in to his assignment and to pledge our life to it, in his name."

The classic image of believing in Jesus is somebody kneeling at an altar and praying, "Oh, God, I'm a sinner, please save me." That's a good start, but that is not an accurate interpretation of Jesus's words to Nicodemus. Jesus was talking to a ruler of the Jewish people, saying "You must leave your religion and enter my kingdom to be born again. The only way you can get into my kingdom is to be born again."

John the Baptist preached: "Repent, for the kingdom of heaven is at hand" (Matthew 3:2). A profound message from an uncomplicated man in camel hair who lived on bugs and honey. *The kingdom of heaven is at hand.* It's right here. It's with us. It's here. John didn't say, "Repent, for a new religion is on the horizon."

John the Baptist was the son of Zechariah—the high priest of his generation. John was in line to fill that high priest position, but he left that lineage for another calling and purpose. From the moment his mother declared a new name for him, one outside of the family names, John was a prophet, a forerunner to Jesus.

> *And it happened that on the eighth day they came to circumcise the child, and they were going to call him Zechariah, after his father. And yet his mother responded and said, "No indeed; but he shall be called John."*
>
> *And they said to her, "There is no one among your relatives who is called by this name."*
>
> *And they made signs to his father, as to what he wanted him called. And he asked for a tablet and wrote as follows, "His name is John."*
>
> Luke 1:59-63

His name was John, as foretold by the angel of the Lord, and he soon realized his calling as a prophet and teacher with a different message. He found his identity through sonship, and he was used by God to prepare the way for Jesus...locusts and all.

> *So he was saying to the crowds who were going out to be baptized by him, "You offspring of vipers, who warned you to flee from the wrath to come? Therefore produce fruits that are consistent with repentance, and do not start saying to yourselves, 'We have Abraham as our father,' for I say to you that from these stones God is able to raise up children for Abraham. But indeed the axe is already being laid at the root of the trees; so every tree that does not bear good fruit is cut down and thrown into the fire."*
>
> Luke 3:7-9

Who was John preaching to at the river Jordan? He was not directing his message to Gentiles, although he did admonish the Roman soldiers who came to him:

> *And the crowds were questioning him, saying, "Then what are we to do?" And he would answer and say to them, "The one who has two tunics is to share with the one who has none; and the one who has food is to do likewise." Now even tax collectors came to be baptized, and they said to him, "Teacher, what are we to do?" And he said to them, "Collect no more than what you have been ordered to." And soldiers also were questioning him, saying, "What are we to do, we as well?" And he said to them, "Do not extort money from anyone, nor harass anyone, and be content with your wages."*
>
> Luke 3:10-14

In fact, John's message was primarily to Abraham's seed, Jewish men whose entire lives were centered on the temple, people who dedicated their lives to God through their religion. These were men who had memorized much of the Old Testament before they were thirteen. And now, here's this wild man in soaking wet camel hair declaring "Repent!" He's calling them a brood of vipers and asserting that "the axe is already being laid at the root of the trees... [to be] cut down and thrown into a fire" (Matthew 3:10).

Incendiary language, to say the least.

You have to wonder, what was it that caused the people to not only tolerate John's insults but to flock to him? Recall our discussion a few pages back, that unlearning must precede learning, and that realizing you don't know something is a prerequisite for acquiring knowledge. The Jews in Israel were under the oppressive boot of Rome. Everything they'd been taught to believe about the preeminence of the Jewish nation lay in ruins. Their lives were ruled by Gentiles, and that rule, though ruthless, was also systematic. The Roman kingdom ruled with oppressive efficiency. You opposed it at your peril.

The Jews were ready for a new hope. They understood John's language in terms of Kingdom. They knew what kingdom was because of the Empire of Rome. Remember earlier from Galatians:

When the fullness of the time had come, God sent forth His Son, born of a woman, born under the law, to redeem those who were under the law, that we might receive the adoption as sons.

Galatians 4:4-5

When that governmental structure was in place, Jesus came into the earth. The Jews knew the language. Jesus and John drew from Greco-Roman culture and used it to establish the foundation of all God was about to do. "The Kingdom of God is at hand (Mark 1:15)." John didn't say a new temple was coming. He said "The kingdom of God is coming. You need to change the way you relate to God." Why? Because their relationship with God had been centered on the temple. That was about to change. God was sending his government into the earth. He was sending his kingdom, not a religion. And to make his point, that temple they loved would be torn down. Not one stone would be left on another.

Some of the Jews got it. Others didn't. Note that even Jesus' disciples expected him to restore the Jewish kingdom.

So, when they had come together, they began asking Him, saying, "Lord, is it at this time that You are restoring the kingdom to Israel?"

Acts 1:16

Still, everyone thought in terms of kingdom. The question was, which kingdom?

John was a Master teacher, a rabbi, of which there were many in the land. He was also a prophet. He preached a message the Jews would not have heard in the temple. John taught a message about the Kingdom of God and a Messiah bringing the Kingdom of God into the earth. "Guys, if you want to identify with this message, if you are willing to believe and to buy into what I'm preaching and teaching about the Kingdom of God, you need to publicly join me."

John's method of initiation? Baptism. "If you want to buy in, you need to dive in."

John's baptism was a baptism of repentance, but not repentance of sin. It was repentance from the way the Jews related to God. It was accepting God's message: "I'm not doing that anymore. Now I'm doing this." Splash!

> If you want to buy in, you need to dive in.

John didn't dunk them and declare: "According to your profession of faith in the Lord Jesus Christ, my brother, I baptize you by the authority given to me in the name of the Father, Son and the Holy Spirit, by the power of Jesus' name. Down we go, up we come."

That is not what John did. That is what we do, but that is not what John did. Instead, his adherents waded into the water and presented themselves to be aligned with John's message. John simply witnessed their baptism.

One day, Jesus the Messiah (also the cousin of John) walked into the river and said, "Baptize me." I imagine about that time, John felt like he was finger-painting in front of Rembrandt. (Yeah, I know Rembrandt wasn't born yet. John was a prophet. He knew things. OK?) Here's the exact transaction:

> Then Jesus arrived from Galilee at the Jordan, coming to John to be baptized by him. But John tried to prevent Him, saying, "I have the need to be baptized by You, and yet You are coming to me?"
>
> But Jesus, answering, said to him, "Allow it at this time; for in this way it is fitting for us to fulfill all righteousness."
>
> Then he allowed Him. After He was baptized, Jesus came up immediately from the water; and behold, the heavens were opened, and he saw the Spirit of God descending as a dove and settling on Him, and behold, a voice from the heavens said, "This is My beloved Son, with whom I am well pleased."
>
> Matthew 3:13-17

Thus, Jesus was baptized into John's baptism, a baptism of repentance. Jesus stepped into the river to be baptized by John like everybody else did—another Jewish man repenting from the temple. That is probably why he got in trouble every time he went into the temple. He turned over heavy stone tables of the merchants and money changers and drove them off with a whip. At age 12, he ditched his parents for three days to engage the scholars in the Jerusalem temple. Now, we need to understand that every twelve-year-old Jewish boy had to know the Torah. But Jesus sat down and brought Father's original intent out of the passages, and it boggled the scholars' minds.

When Jesus walked into the river, John said something powerful, for the Jewish people of that culture knew what the Lamb signified.

> *The next day John saw Jesus coming toward him, and said, "Behold! The Lamb of God who takes away the sin of the world!"*
>
> John 1:29

"Takes away the sin of...." what? Not your sins, or my sins. The sin of "the world." When John identified Jesus as the Messiah, it was not a religious term. Messiah is a governmental term. It means "ruler, king, anointed one." The Jews were not looking for a rabbi; they were looking for a king. Jesus was identified by John as the Lamb of God, the sacrifice that would be made. He was the one who would take away the "sin of the world." *Sin*, as in singular, not *sins*, as in plural. That sin takes us back to the Garden and the fall. The word *sin* means "rebellion" in Greek. It doesn't mean: "Oh, I did a bad thing. I'm a rotten person. Oh, Lord, please cleanse me." No, saying we sinned means we rebelled.

Sin in the Hebrew ties to the word *treason*, as when we do something against a nation. Adam committed treason in the Garden. He rebelled. Remember, Adam did not lose a religion in the Garden. He lost *radah*. He lost rulership, he lost kingdom, he lost authority, he lost government in the Garden.

Satan wanted to give Jesus the kingdoms of the world if he would worship him. Jesus didn't worship him. Jesus obtained them God's way: through his death, burial and resurrection.

Jesus was solid in his identity. Jesus knew who he was and what he was on earth to do: take away the sin of the world. He was reestablishing order in the earth, restoring the *kosmos*: governmental structure, governmental authority, governmental order, and kingdom.

If we believe in Jesus, we will live eternally in his kingdom. Ours is citizenship, not membership. Membership in a church does not guarantee access to the kingdom. Only citizenship guarantees access to the kingdom.

As an American citizen, I carry an American passport, and that passport has power associated with it. It doesn't look powerful—just a booklet with a bunch of stamps and the picture of an awesome-looking guy. But when it is presented in the right places, it opens nations to me. Now, my wife, Joan (pronounced "Jo-ann"), was born in the Philippines. When she married me, she came to the United States and got a green card, and that gave her limited access to the country. She could come and go, move around the country, and hold a job. Yet she couldn't vote. She couldn't make governmental decisions. Why? Because she was still a Filipino citizen.

Many church people today are still citizens of another kingdom; all they have is a green card. They can move around the church, but they have no governmental authority. It wasn't until Joan applied for citizenship, learned about our Constitution and history, recited the Pledge of Allegiance and passed a test on all these things, that she was eligible for citizenship. Remarkably, legal immigrants today know a lot more about our country than native-born citizens do. But when Joan raised her right hand, she pledged allegiance to the United States of America and said her oath to this nation: "I will defend it against enemies, foreign and domestic." In that moment, she gave her heart to this nation to become a U.S. citizen. And the government official said: "Welcome to America. You are now a United States citizen."

They gave her an American passport. Now, she can vote and make governmental decisions. She can do anything a citizen can do, and sometimes even do it better. She even ran for the State House in Hawaii...twice! Religion will give you a "Green Card" which allows you very limited access. Kingdom gives you a passport, which grants you full access to all the Kingdom of God possesses.

Citizenship is the perfect picture of what Jesus told Nicodemus. "You must be born again." Those who believe, those who buy into his purpose and accept his assignment, actually leave one nation and enter another. Remember, a kingdom is a nation. It is a country. We leave one kingdom and come into another Kingdom. We leave the

Kingdom of Darkness and come into the Kingdom of Light. We switch citizenship. It is a legal act, not an emotional alliance. My wife doesn't have to feel like an American; she is an American. (She can even eat her dried, stinky fish and rice—a Philippine delicacy.) We take for granted a lot of things that our citizenship bestows upon us. We do the same regarding the Kingdom of God. We have to rediscover those things...and we will!

5

Reestablishing Identity

SONSHIP ACCORDING TO THE KINGDOM is different than sonship according to religion. This is why, to become a son, everything that is out of place in our lives needs to be reestablished. We need to understand that we are sons and daughters, through and through.

The enemy will try to defeat this process. "Oh, well, maybe that's for somebody else. You just can't overcome. You can't make it. You're struggling here, struggling there."

Well, Jesus struggled too. The Bible says we do not have a high priest who cannot be touched with the feelings of our infirmities, but likewise, in all manners, he was tempted like we are, yet without sin. Isn't that amazing?

> *Seeing then that you have a great High Priest who has passed through the heavens, Jesus the Son of God, let us hold fast our confession. For we do not have a High Priest who cannot sympathize with our weaknesses, but was in all points tempted as we are, yet without sin. Let us therefore come boldly to the throne of grace, that we may obtain mercy and find grace to help in time of need.*
>
> Hebrews 4:14-16

The responsibility of the five-fold gifts to the Church is to bring us into the fullness of Christ. Part of that process is suffering. Interestingly, that is not preached anymore. Preach on suffering and watch the offerings drop to nothing. So instead, we are taught not to expect trials, troubles, tribulations, and if they do happen, it's a sure sign that we are not living right.

The truth is, difficulty is probably a sign that we are doing our best to live for the Lord, and now we are making our way through some junk that is coming to the surface because we are pressing into God. Of course, we don't dwell in our difficulties. We don't even endure in the aspects of being stuck, but we make our way through those things. We are pushing through. We all have trials, but we are moving to victory. We don't live from a place of struggle or defeat. We live from the victory of our risen King!

Think of it this way: when an athlete trains, he's not trying to prove how strong he is. No, he's trying to find out how weak he is. *What's my endurance? When do I fail?* Why would he want to know that? So, he knows where to focus his training. Pressing into God highlights the weak areas of ourselves so we can work with God to make those areas stronger. Huuuaaah!

James, the brother of Jesus, said that we are to endure trials and tribulations:

> *Consider it all joy, my brothers and sisters, when you encounter various trials, knowing that the testing of your faith produces endurance. And let endurance have its perfect result, so that you may be perfect and complete, lacking in nothing.*
>
> James 1:2-4

> **It is not a sign that we are defeated. It is a sign that we are dangerous.**

Now, James is not telling us to stay in the struggle. Like a runner who practices marathons, we develop the stamina to push through trials and tribulations that we go through in life. It is not a sign that we are defeated. It is a sign that we are dangerous. The enemy never bothers things that don't threaten him. We know we are a threat when he comes after us.

Reestablishing Identity

These things I [Jesus] have spoken to you so that in Me you may have peace. In the world you have tribulation, but take courage; I have overcome the world.

John 16:33

God's end goal for us is peace, and the process is tribulation. He has not left us defenseless. We are learning to overcome.

We are of God, little children, and have overcome them, because He who is in you is greater than he who is in the world.

1 John 4:4

Sonship is not a membership process. It is a citizenship process. In the Kingdom of God, all the citizens are sons and daughters. There are no second-class citizens. There are no citizens trying to become sons and daughters. We are the children of God, and we are growing and maturing into partners with God.

WHAT IS INHERITANCE?

As we step into sonship, we receive our inheritance. What is our inheritance? Money? Land? Our parents spoiled little K-9 who loses its mind when the Amazon truck pulls into the driveway? No. Inheritance is everything that we need for our assignment. Everything we need for our assignment is included in our inheritance.

> Everything we need for our assignment is included in our inheritance.

Many have been taught that inheritance is wealth. The church went through that phase with the charismatic movement. We went through the "name it and claim it" stuff. Leaders told us to go down to the car dealership, lay our hands on our Cadillac and claim it in the name of Jesus. Yeah, we better claim the payments, too, and a better job.

Because if that Cadillac doesn't belong in our life, if that is not a part of our assignment, it will wind up being a dead weight.

Joan and I learned that when God wants us to have things we need for our assignment, he provides them. There have been times in our lives when there were things that we knew we needed for our assignment, but we got ahead of God and got them on our own. Guess what? We lost them. Why? Because we got them before God gave them to us. We went out to get "ours." *This is mine. I need this thing for my assignment. I need this for the ministry. What's wrong with that?* We've all done that in some form or fashion. There are things that I thought I needed, so I went and got them. But I didn't need them at that time, nor did I have the release from God that it was okay to get them at that time.

When we obtain things, thinking they're ours, we also incur the responsibility of maintaining them. Whether it is a vehicle, a house, land, a building, a ring, a relationship, whatever it may be...if we were never told by God to have it, we're in trouble. We essentially get things "illegitimately." Even though God wants us to have them, we are in trouble when we get out ahead of God and his provision. We find ourselves with illegitimate things and positions we never should have had because we went ahead of God.

In Luke 4, the enemy presented to Jesus all the kingdoms of the world and offered them to him. Satan had a legal right to give them to Jesus. Recall the essence of Jesus' reply to this temptation: "I'm going to get them, but I'm not going to get them right now. I'm going to take them, but I'm going through the process to get them according to the way my Father wants to deliver them to me." Jesus knew he was going to die. But he also knew that when he rose, he was going to get those kingdoms back.

> *And Jesus [after his resurrection] came and spoke to them, saying, "All authority has been given to Me in heaven and on earth.*
>
> Matthew 28:18

Jesus said: "Now all *exousia* (Greek), all power, all authority has been given to me." Where? "In heaven and on earth."

GET UP

The heaven Jesus was talking about was not what we have been taught. Jesus never lost authority in the third heaven where God dwells. Paul referred to the three levels of heaven when he said:

> *I know a man in Christ, who fourteen years ago—whether in the body I do not know, or out of the body I do not know, God knows—such a man was caught up to the third heaven.*
>
> 2 Corinthians 12

The third heaven is where we find the throne of God. It is not actually up, as in a physical position. Rather, it is up as in another realm. Heaven is not way out there somewhere in the sweet by and by. Heaven is very near to us; it is all around us; it is the air we breathe.

In Job, we read:

> *If He [God] were to gather*
> *His spirit and His breath to Himself,*
> *Humanity would perish together,*
> *And mankind would return to dust.*
>
> Job 34:14

Hebrew culture knew this. The natural and the supernatural are integral to each other. The false teaching that a line of separation exists demarking the earth below (natural) and heaven above (supernatural) was an attempt by Greek philosophers to account for the condition of sin they saw among mankind.

We need a new definition of "up."

> *After these things I looked, and behold, a door standing open in heaven. And the first voice which I heard was like a trumpet speaking with me, saying, "Come up here, and I will show you things which must take place after this."*
>
> Revelation 4:1

God told John to "Come up here." John was caught up into heaven and saw things that were coming. Jesus wasn't talking about that heaven in Matthew 28:18.

There are three heavens. There is our heaven—the atmosphere that we live in. There is the second heaven, described in the book of Daniel as a place where the prince and the power of the air dwelled. In Daniel 10, Daniel prayed, and God released the answer immediately through the angel Gabriel. Yes, Gabriel was sent, but he was held up in the heavenlies by the Prince of Persia. This wasn't a physical man; it was a principality, the satanic prince that ruled over that region in the heavenlies. Gabriel fought him for 21 days.

> Then he said to me, "Do not be afraid, Daniel, for from the first day that you set your heart on understanding this and on humbling yourself before your God, your words were heard, and I have come in response to your words. But the prince of the kingdom of Persia was standing in my way for twenty-one days; then behold, Michael, one of the chief princes, came to help me, for I had been left there with the kings of Persia.
>
> Daniel 10:12-13

The word *prince* means "ruler, first ruler, one with authority, realm." On the 21st day, God sent the archangel Michael to help fight this prince. Gabriel was finally released, and he brought Daniel his answer. God had answered him the first day. Gabriel had just been held up in the second heaven.

The good news is that Jesus reclaimed his authority in the second heaven. He already had it in the third heaven. He regained it in the first heaven (earth) and in the second heaven.

HELL, WHO NEEDS IT?

Jesus regained authority in all created things through his death, burial, resurrection, and ascension. Today, he is sitting at the right hand of the Father (ref. Hebrews 10:12-13). God created the planets, the stars, the moon, the sun. He did not lease that space out to the devil. The enemy has no authority there. He also has no authority here on the earth unless a man gives it to him. Since the resurrection and ascension of Jesus, Satan has no power, voice or authority in the earth *unless* a man or a woman gives him an opening to a seat of authority.

That is the good news to us as sons and daughters. Religion tells us the devil is the prince of this world. Folks: he is not the prince of this world. He was dethroned by the resurrection. Glory to God! Jesus defeated death, he defeated hell, and he defeated the grave. Amen. As a matter of fact, Satan is an unemployed cherub. He does not own hell. He's not looking forward to going to hell. He's not throwing a party in hell. His demons are not running around tormenting people in hell. Satan is not in charge of hell. Yes, Milton quoted Satan in *Paradise Lost*: "Better to reign in Hell than serve in Heaven." Guess what? Milton was a poet, not a theologian. Satan doesn't rule anywhere, not on earth and sure as hell not in...ah, you get it.

Still, religion and pop culture tell us the devil is in charge of hell. That's not in scripture. The Bible says Satan will be thrown into the lake of fire. Satan isn't happy about it. I can't say I blame him. Forever is a long time, especially toward the end.

Jesus owns hell. David said in Psalm 139:8, "If I make my bed in hell, behold, you are there." God owns hell, and he owns everything to do with the operation of hell. *Why? Because he pays the gas bill?* No. The fact is, hell was not created for man. It was created for the devil and his angels. It is a place of punishment for these fallen cherubs to be tormented for eternity.

Man is never sent to hell by God. Man goes to hell by an act of his own will in rejecting God. People say: "Well, if he was a loving God, he would never send anybody to hell." That's true. God has never sent anyone to hell.

Jesus took back everything in creation. That is why you and I have everything in creation that we need to fulfill our assignment as sons and daughters. Everything we need is already available to us. As we

> We are birthed into the Kingdom of God as children, and we grow into sonship.

read in Galatians 4, it is released to us according to our maturity. Remember: *son* means, "mature one." This adoption process is not something that happens when we are born again. When we are born again, we become a child of God. We are birthed into the kingdom. The adoption process is when we grow and mature until the Father pulls us into his side and tells all of those in our realm: "He is now a partner in the family business." We are birthed into the Kingdom of God as children, and we grow into sonship.

RETURNING TO THE SOURCE

In Luke 15, we find the famous parable about a man who had two sons. Now, that was trouble right there, because it necessitated splitting the inheritance. In Jewish culture, you did not have to wait until your father died to receive an inheritance. Legacy and inheritance were intended to advance the next generation. It was never intended for the next generation to take their piece and run off with it. It was a matter of stewardship. When he was ready, a son was given a portion of the family wealth to manage in order to grow the family.

In a family with multiple sons, the oldest son took the inheritance and distributed it. He gave responsibility to the other sons in the family to steward parts of the land and wealth. When there were only two sons, however, the oldest was not the distributor of the inheritance. Instead, the wealth was divided equally among the two sons.

Let's look at Luke 15:11-32. I am going to paraphrase the story to emphasize key points.

A man had two sons. The younger of them demanded of his father: "Father, give me my share of the estate." So, the father divided his wealth between his two sons.

Reestablishing Identity

A few days later, the younger son gathered everything together and went out on a journey into a distant country. In so doing, he entered a different kingdom. There he squandered his estate, partying like a rock star. After he spent everything, a severe famine occurred in that nation. Faced with starvation, he hired himself out to the citizens of that kingdom. They sent him into the fields to feed the pigs, where he would have gladly filled his stomach with the food the swine were eating.

Now, Jews were not supposed to have anything to do with pigs, so he wasn't within the Jewish culture in this distant land. He had journeyed to a nation of defilement. The swine were eating well, and he was wasting away.

When he finally came to his senses—funny how hunger does that—he said:

> *How many of my father's hired laborers have more than enough bread, but I am dying here from hunger! I will set out and go to my father, and will say to him, "Father, I have sinned against heaven, and in your sight; I am no longer worthy to be called your son; treat me as one of your hired laborers."*
>
> Luke 15:17-19

So, he journeyed to his father, and while he was still a long way off, Daddy saw him and was filled with compassion. He ran and embraced his boy—his boney, pig-smelling boy in rags—and he kissed him.

The son uttered the lines he'd been rehearsing since his journey started: "Father, I have sinned against heaven and in your sight. I am no longer worthy to be called your son." But the father ignored him and said to his servants: "Quickly bring out the best robe and put it on him. Put a ring on his hand and sandals on his feet. Kill the fatted calf and let's celebrate. For this son of mine, who was dead, has come to life again. He was lost and has been found."

And they begin to celebrate.

Great story, right? (Unless you're the fatted calf.) Now, let's switch perspectives to the son. The term *father* in Hebrew culture meant "source." It didn't just mean the man who got mom pregnant. It meant the person who was the source both of life and everything in life.

In the Kingdom of God, our heavenly Father is our source. It is not our job, education, gifts nor talents. Our heavenly Father should be the totality of our source. Everything starts with and is sustained through him.

This young man made a fateful decision in life. He came to the source and demanded his share of the estate—that which belonged to the family; to the estate; that portion he was supposed to steward for the benefit of all. Now, the word *estate* is the word *periousia* in Greek. It comes from the word *execution*, which is "authority," and it is derived from the Greek word *ousia*. It means "substance, property, fortune, holdings." He was asking his *source* for his portion of the estate.

In like manner, our identity today is tied to our heavenly Father's estate. Why? Because our Father does not rent things. He owns things. Kingdom is our family business. Our Father is not a cobbler, a carpenter, a bus driver, a plumber; he's not a doctor, a lawyer, a theologian or a preacher. He is a king. He has a vast estate called earth.

> *The earth is the Lord's, and all it contains,*
> *The world, and those who live in it.*
>
> Psalm 24:1

Just as this young man approached his earthly source, Jesus knew that his heavenly Father was his source. Jesus drew from his Father as his source. We see this from his last words on the cross:

> *And Jesus, crying out with a loud voice, said, "Father, into Your hands I entrust My spirit." And having said this, He died.*
>
> Luke 23:46

It's as if he was saying: "Father, I am giving my spirit into your hands as I step into death. You are my source of resurrection into life."

With God as his source, Jesus understood himself as the resurrection and the life.

> "I am the resurrection and the life; the one who believes in Me will live, even if he dies, and everyone who lives and believes in Me will never die.
>
> John 11:25-26

In that moment of death, he was declaring to the Father: "I am giving myself back to you. I am depositing my life back into your hands. You are my source of life."

Jesus knew he was not the resurrection and the life without the Father. His ability to be the resurrection and the life was an impartation of what Father had already given to him as an inheritance.

RELIGIOUS VS KINGDOM THINKING

Kingdom tells us that our heavenly Father is our source for everything. He is our Jehovah-Jireh, our provider.

Religion tells us that God sees our need and has pity on us; that somehow, we might get a little favor from him. Maybe he'll drop a breadcrumb into our life to sustain us for the moment. Religious thinking prays: "God, meet my need."

Kingdom thinking prays: "God, we have a problem, and we need a solution. You, me and we, God.

Religion says: "God I have a problem. Would you please have compassion on me? Would you please move in my life? God, would you please meet this need? Would you pay my rent this month? Would you pay my car payment? God, would you help me keep the electricity on?" That is religious thinking.

Kingdom says: "Father, the estate's electric bill is due. How do you want to take care of this?"

It all comes down to stewardship and maturity. As we are faithful with the little, he entrusts us with much. We don't just go to God and say: "God, you need to pay my bills." No. It is a partnership; one in which we must be proven to steward resources well.

This young man in Jesus' parable came to his source and said: "I want to divide the estate. I want what's mine."

Now, this word *estate* in the Greek (1510 in Strong's) means, "I exist, I am." So, in essence, he was saying: "Give me my portion of my existence." See, his existence was tied up in the estate. His existence was his purpose. It was the answer to the deep questions we all ask ourselves: *Why am I here? What is my goal? What is my purpose for living?* He decided to answer those apart from the source, separating from the father and the family estate. It didn't work out too well for him, but...such is youth. It is our opportunity to make mistakes and learn from them before we are too old to make any more.

WHAT IS OUR BENT?

Many people today do not know their purpose in life. They are tied up into a religion that says: "Serve me!" They need to be tied into an estate that bestows sonship. We ask children all the time: "What do you want to be when you grow up?"

One day, they want to be a fireman. The next day, they want to drive a garbage truck. In a week, they'll want to be a preacher. (Sounds like they're on the right track.) They have all these ideas, but the word of God never tells us to leave it up to our children to discover who they are. That is not how the Kingdom of God operates. Rather, we are to train our children in *the way they should go*.

> *Train up a child in the way he should go,*
> *Even when he grows older he will not abandon it.*
>
> Proverbs 22:6

Yeah, that's pretty good advice, and it's in the Bible, but how well do we understand it? What is: "the way he should go"? Religion would

Reestablishing Identity

say: train them to go to church, sing in the choir, drop a few coins in the plate, and take the family to IHOP once in a while. But it's deeper than that. It always is.

A better understanding of this phrase is to train a child in the way he is created by God. This is better, but it requires an intimate knowledge of what God has called the child to do and be. Well, when left to his own devices, what is the child inclined to do? As we pray and observe, we will get an idea of the direction God intends for his offspring. And then, we have another task—to cultivate that which God has endowed to this child, so that when he is old, he will walk in God's purpose and not depart from it.

Instead of asking our children what they want to be when they grow up, we should pray with them, prophesy over them, and decree into their lives all that God has called them to be. Parents are graced by God to know what their children are called to do. But religion has told us: "Just pray that they will follow Jesus when they are grown. That they will have a heart for God, serve the church and be good Christians."

I know a father, Matt, whose son is a one-year-old. That boy loves noise, so Matt got him a drum set for Christmas. The boy loves to beat the drums and clang the symbols, at times with a discernable rhythm. So, now Matt and his son sit together and watch videos of drummers. Why? Because Matt knows part of his son's assignment in life is music. He is willing to endure the novice drummer, all the bangs and clangs, the late-night jam sessions while binging on formula. It'll all be worth it someday. And then, maybe Matt can get some sleep.

My parents gave me a drum set when I was in the 6th grade. They set it up in the living room. I had an eight-piece drum set, and I went at it every day. I was in there for hours playing that drum set, and I thought I was making some beautiful music. In time, I learned to play the drums fairly well.

And then one day I had a boy of my own, Micah, (the one on the front cover of this book), and he wanted a drum kit. He would stand beside me while I played. I thought: *oh man, this is cute. It is good to have my boy stand beside me when I play.* Micah started climbing on the drum stool when I was away. Next thing I knew, he wanted a set of drums like daddy, so I got him a set. It was then that I understood the hell my parents endured when I was learning to play. Apparently, there is no statute of limitations to "we reap what we sow."

But my parents knew I had music in me, so they did everything they could do to encourage that music out of me. My dad was a hall-of-fame musician who came from a musical family and taught us to play as a band. We played for Ronald Reagan in the Rotunda Room of the White House. Now, we weren't just invited because we were cute kids. We were invited because we had won every talent show throughout the mid-south area. We had competed against musicians from all over the country, and we won. On our way home from Washington D.C., however, the group broke up. That was the will of God. He had other plans for me. But music was a big part of it.

Later in life, Joan, the children and I planted many churches in the United States and other nations. Often, we were the musicians for worship. Micah played the drums. I played keyboard. Joan led worship. (No, Daddy didn't sing bass. And little brother? We fired him 'cause he wouldn't join right in there.)

I Did It My Way

So, this young man in Jesus' parable was not living in his God-given gifts and calling. He wanted to develop himself his own way. "I want my own purpose. 'I am' is my identity. I want to define me. I want to be my own man. I want my independence. I want to live on my own."

Funny how everybody wants to be on their own until it's time to pay the bills. They want the freedom of being independent, but they still want that umbilical cord tied to the family wallet. "I want my own ideas. I want to develop who I am. And I want the family estate to finance it."

In sonship, we develop through the family estate, but we operate through the family purpose. Jesus spoke of himself saying: "I and *the Father* are one." Jesus never insinuated that he wanted to be his own man.

That they all may be one, as You, Father, are in Me, and I in You.

John 17:21 NKJV

The true Lord's Prayer is John 17. (Matthew 6 should be called the Disciples' Prayer.) Jesus was vested in the estate of the earth. Our identity should not come through our own independence but through our interdependence upon our source—our heavenly Father.

The young man wanted to create his own purpose. He wanted to pull away from the source and forge his own path.

The word *estate* also means, "to belong." He said, "I want to create my own tribe. I don't want to belong to this estate any longer. I want to be able to do my own thing, create my own way, have my own identity."

As I studied this topic, I began to see this in my life. This led to repentance: *Father, forgive me for independence. I don't want to build my own ministry anymore. I don't have a ministry. I am vested in the estate. Amen.* We all must give an account for the things God gives to us. Why? Because he didn't give them in the sense that they're ours to use as we choose. They are given to us to steward; to use wisely to expand the family business.

Our assignment is not to build our own ministry. I cringe when people refer to ministry as *my church. Hey, how's your church doing?* It is not your church. It is Jesus' church. We have merely been given stewardship over it.

Another word for *ousia,* translated "estate" in scripture, is "done, finished, complete." When we are vested in the estate of God—when we are vested into everything he's doing, then everything is done. It is complete, finished. If we pull away, we depart from something that has already been completed.

This young man said: "I want you to give me what belongs to me. I don't want to be under the source anymore. I want ownership."

The word *estate* also means "access." So, the son was saying: "I want to move from access to ownership. I want to own things instead of having access to them."

This is in stark contrast to what Jesus told his disciples:

But when He, the Spirit of truth, comes, He will guide you into all the truth; for He will not speak on His own, but whatever He hears, He will speak; and He will disclose to you what is to come. He will glorify Me, for He will take from Mine and will disclose it to you. All things that the Father has are Mine; this is why I said that He takes from Mine and will disclose it to you.

John 16:13-15 NASB

Jesus said: "Everything the Father has is mine. And when Holy Spirit comes, he's going to take of mine and disclose it to you. The Father is my source. Everything the Father has is mine. You don't have to leave the kingdom to have it. In fact, if you leave, you could lose...everything."

In the kingdom of God, *mine* is a dangerous word. In Religion, *mine* is an important word. When we say *mine* and *yours*, it creates competition among us. *Mine is better than yours. My church is bigger than yours. How many did y'all baptized this year? In mine, we baptized 100. Oh yeah? Well, in mine we baptized 102. What now, creep? Glory to God!*

In the kingdom, when we take ownership of something, we lose it. This young man in Jesus' parable wanted to move from access to ownership. He soon discovered that everything he got from the source was gone. He had to hire himself out as a citizen in another country; he sold himself to another system. Remember, there are only two kingdoms: light and darkness. He went from access to ownership to *lights out Amigo*.

The fact is, we own nothing. We are not supposed to own anything. God owns all my money. None of it is my money. People say: "I gave my tithe." No, you didn't give your tithe. You returned to God his portion of the partnership. When we tithe, we haven't given God anything. We might think we gave God something when we tithe. The truth is, we are a partner in the family business. We have just returned to him his portion. He said the first 10% is his and we take the 90%. Hopefully, we steward it together to expand God's kingdom. Tithing is not even under the Levitical structure. It is under the order of Melchizedek—the new priesthood. We give him a tenth of all that we have, not just money, but our time, our possessions, everything. Why? Because it is all his anyway. We are just stewarding these things to further his kingdom.

Tithing is empowerment. It reinforces the partnership that we have with the Father in the family business. It is not to be done under compulsion. If we don't tithe, God is not going to whip us; we will not have holes in our pockets. No, that is Levitical thinking. We tithe under the Melchizedek priesthood, not under the Levitical priesthood. Melchizedek operated from the power of an endless life comprised of an eternal source, an everlasting supply. He sat down with Abraham who took back his family. Abraham freed Lot from bondage, and then he earned a name, a reputation, and he gained authority in the regions of kings. Abraham was not engaged in anything until then. He had to go fight to get his family back. And when he did, Melchizedek came and sat with him. Abraham took a tithe of the spoil and gave it to Melchizedek.

ESTATE OWNERSHIP

This young man in Jesus' parable was desperate for his destiny, so he hired himself out as a citizen of another country. He removed himself from the structure of kingdom and set himself back into the structure of slavery. It is as we read in Galatians 4:

> *But now that you have come to know God, or rather to be known by God, how is it that you turn back again to the weak and worthless elementary principles, to which you want to be enslaved all over again?*
>
> Galatians 4:9

We each have an inheritance. We must figure out what God has called us to do. We must find our identity in the estate. It starts with saying: "I exist for the Father. I am for the Father."

Moses asked God: "Who do I tell them sent me when I go to the sons of Israel? God replied: "Tell them that I AM WHO I AM sent me. Tell Pharaoh the estate sent you."

> *Then Moses said to God, "Indeed, when I come to the children of Israel and say to them, 'The God of your fathers has sent me to you,' and they say to me, 'What is His name?' what shall I say to them?"*
>
> *And God said to Moses, "I AM WHO I AM." And He said, "Thus you shall say to the children of Israel, 'I AM has sent me to you.'"*
>
> Exodus 3:13-14 NKJV

When we take that phrase, "I AM WHO I AM ... has sent me," and interpret it through a religious lens, we end up with a riddle. *Who is he that he is? The I am that I am?* Kingdom understands what God was saying. Moses was to tell Pharaoh that the estate owner had arrived. Pharaoh understood this language as God intended. A riddle would not have intimidated Pharaoh. But when we represent the estate, saying the owner has arrived and wants his property back—that which Pharoah currently has in his possession—it sheds a different light on that matter. The source says he wants it back, so turn it loose Pharaoh. It's not a matter of *if you return it*; it's a matter of *when you return it*, and more to the point: *the price of your delay*. That's kingdom.

Moses was operating governmentally. He was not there as a religious priest. He was there as a king, a ruler. "The estate owner wants his property back. Let it go."

And Pharaoh said: "Nope, I am not letting it go."

"All right, Pharaoh. You get another night with the frogs because the estate wants its property back."

"No, I'm keeping it."

"All right, here come some locusts. It is going to cost you if you are holding property that belongs to another estate, especially this King's estate. You are going to lose all your crops. You will be riddled with plagues until you decide to let it go."

All of that came upon Egypt as Pharaoh remained stubborn. It finally came down to: "Now it is going to cost you your family. It is going to cost you your firstborn. It is going to cost you your throne, the person who is to carry on after you. It will cost you the authority in your country. You are going to lose everything because you are holding property that belongs to another estate—the *I AM* estate."

Knowing that Pharaoh was ready to break, Moses told the Israelites: "Put blood on your doorpost because the estate is sending death through the country. And if blood is on your doorpost, it will pass over you. It will not come into your houses because it will know you are in covenant with the estate."

This is kingdom; this is government.

Of course, we know the story. The firstborn of every Egyptian household died and Pharaoh had had enough. "Take all of Israel and go! Take my gold with you. Take my jewels with you. Take everything and get out of my country."

And so, they did.

No Going Back

The young man in Jesus' parable who had decided to leave the estate and enter the darkness of slavery became a victim of the system. He surrendered his portion of stewardship of the estate, bought into the system of the world, and ended up stealing slop from the pigs. This was more than sharing communion with pigs. This young man was put into an environment that totally defiled him as a son of the estate. Pigs were one of the nastiest things on the planet for a Jew. They couldn't touch them; they couldn't be around them; they couldn't own them. Remember, Jesus cast the devils out of a man, ordered the demons into the pigs, and the pigs ran off a cliff and drowned. Smart pigs, huh? The owners, who were Jews, got mad at Jesus, who responded: "You are not supposed to be owning pigs. Why are you mad?"

They were doing something that was outside the culture. We surrender ourselves to things many times that are outside the culture of the Kingdom of God. This is tragic. When we are tied to the source through adoption, every need is supplied. We don't have to go back into the Kingdom of Darkness looking for provision, identity, or purpose. Everything we need is on our Father's estate. We just have to remain on the estate.

> Everything we need is on our father's estate. We just have to remain on the estate.

Notice something here. The young man surrendered his identity, his purpose and his swords—his means of protection. He went into another country and sold himself into slavery when he lost everything. When we are an owner, it is all gone when we make a mistake. But when we have access, it is still all there, held in reserve for our return. Yet think about this: the father—the source—never went looking for the son who left. It's as if the father knew the son would have to come to his senses on his own. That's a wise father.

SELF EXAMINATION

The Bible says the young man came to himself. This is an important life lesson. When we are in trouble through choices we have made, we must come to ourselves first. The first step to freedom is self-visitation. That young man had to have a conversation with himself. He had to say: "Self, what are you doing here?" It was the right question to lead him back to his father.

Often, people who are bound with religion pray prayers such as: "God, help me get out of here." Well, that's the wrong prayer. The prayer should be: "Father, why am I here?"

If we are asking God to get us out of there, and God is not getting us out of there—whatever "there" might be—we may become angry and frustrated with God. But when we find ourselves stuck in some "there," it is usually because we have left the source. I am not saying we are backsliding—that's a religious term—but we may be in that area of our life where we have pulled away from the source and chosen instead to do our own thing.

The young man needed to have a conversation with himself. What does this tell us? That we cannot go to other people before we go to ourselves.

"I need help, preacher. I need help real bad. Can y'all help me?"

"Well, have you had a conversation with yourself yet?"

This young man started conversing with himself. Good thing he was in with the pigs; anyone else would have thought him crazy.

Prodigal: "Pigs, what's wrong with me?"

Pigs: GRUNT!

Prodigal: "No, really, what's my problem?"

Pigs: GRUNT!

Prodigal: "Oh, so you're saying I need more grunt?"

Pigs: OINK!

Prodigal: "Oh, now I get it. You're saying oikos! That's the Greek word for 'family.' You're saying I need to get back to my family!"

Pigs: GRUNT! OINK!

Prodigal: "Thank you, pigs. You know...you guys should write a book someday."

See, when we're in the pig pen, there are only two types of people we can go to. One type is the people who are in the same pig pen as we are. The trouble with this is we should never discuss our problems with people who are not capable of helping us change. We don't need a pity party. We need a way out. If they knew a way out, they'd be gone already.

When we understand that we are part of the estate—that we have an inheritance and God wants to do things with our lives—we find that he has purposed us, given us identity, and equipped us to accomplish our mission. All we have to do is grow up, catch his vision and partner with him. Maybe not all at once, but returning home is a good way to restart the process. And that is not the advice we are going to get from our partners in pig pen purgatory.

The only other person available when we're in the pig pen is the guy we're working for: the pig farmer. And he is not going to counsel us out of the pen. No siree. He is going to say: "Look man, you are a good pig slopper. Nobody slops pigs like you. You're doing a wonderful job. The pigs love you! Even God loves you. Clearly, he has put you here to slop pigs, man. Look at the facts: bloom where you're planted. Get back in there and slop those pigs to the glory of God!

Before you know it, you're right back in the pen, shoveling slop and hoping he was only kidding about the last part.

When you find yourself in a pig pen; when you're trying to return to the culture and country you were birthed in; when you're in desperate need for a homecoming to the family estate, don't talk to anybody around you. Talk to yourself and God.

In the parable, we do not have any record of anybody from the father's estate coming by that place. Instead, the young man commanded himself. "All right, I will arise." And so, he arose.

We do not need counseling all the time. We don't need to run to pastor: "Pastor, I have this problem." We don't need to chase the prophets and ask: "Do you have a word for me?" Often, we have not obeyed the last "word" we received from a prophet.

People are looking for excuses to not do things that they need to do. This young man said: "I will arise. I am getting myself up." He picked himself up and then he said: "I am going to enter something that will have no limits. I am limited here in this pig pen. My food is pig slop. My neighbors are pigs. Pretty soon, my girlfriend's gonna be a pig. Somebody owns me, and I can't do anything else. I can't even eat what the pigs eat without permission from the pig farmer. I am getting myself up and moving out of this pig pen. I am going to enter back into something that is limitless, that is established. I am going back to the source's house; I am going back to my father's estate, even if it's as a servant. Glory to God."

We need to get back to the estate, back to our source. When we see something and think: *I need that for my ministry. I need that for my assignment and my purpose in the earth. I need to check in with the banker.* No, you do not need the bank down the street or across town. They'll just deny you. They are the pig farmers. Why? Because whenever we go into debt with them, they own us. We are going to be the lender, not the borrower (Deuteronomy. 15:6).

RESTORATION

We need to reattach ourselves to Father's estate and understand that it is not our responsibility to make our own way. It is our responsibility to grow, mature, submit, obey and stay in our lane. When we get sleepy, lose attention and begin weaving into the other lanes, we end up wrecking other lives and ours, too. Stay in our lane. Why? Because we are graced there. We need to recognize the sphere of influence God has given us. What grace has he put upon our life? Where is our fruit coming from? We need to get into that place and stay in that place. Let's stop looking at other people; it only fosters pride or envy. *I want to be like that one. I want to preach like that guy. I want to have a business like this. I want to be like so and so.* No, we don't.

> *And he arose and came to his father. But when he was still a great way off, his father saw him and had compassion, and ran and fell on his neck and kissed him. And the son said to him, 'Father, I have sinned against heaven and in your sight, and am no longer worthy to be called your son.'*
>
> Luke 15:20-21 NKJV

When the father saw his son coming from afar off, he ran to meet him. Notice the son had made his way back, *then* the father came.

James 4:8 says, "Draw near to God and He will draw near to you." Who draws first? We do. When we say: "God, come get me out of my mess," God doesn't hear us. If we are a baby, he will pick us up, wash us off and help us. But if we are someone who wants to move, expand and be victorious in our lives, God is looking for us to make some moves toward him. He said: "If you draw near to me, I will draw near to you." That literally means in the Greek: "If God sees a flicker of our hearts in his direction, he will run to us." Amazing!

The father saw his son coming from afar off. That tells us he was watching. He was looking, maybe standing on the porch, searching. *Is my boy headed this way today? Is my son coming this way today?* God is looking for you. He isn't mad at you. He is expecting you. Glory! The father ran out and met him. He put his arms around his son and hugged him. His son went through the sales pitch.

"Father, source, if you will let me come back to work here like a servant, could I just do that? I know I wronged you. I know I sinned against you and the estate. Would you let me be a servant?"

That's religion talking.

Many people come to God saying: "I know I have sinned, God. I know I have backslid. I know I did all those rotten things, but would you just let me be a servant in your house? Would you have mercy on me, Lord? Would you let me go there? Would you restore my life? Just come back into my heart. Religion tells us to approach God with a pitiful, servant, orphan mentality that keeps us in a position of defeat even when we are on Daddy's porch.

Reestablishing Identity

But the father said to his servants, "Bring out the best robe and put it on him and put a ring on his hand and sandals on his feet."

Luke 15:22

The father turned to his servant and said: "Bring out my robe for him." He was literally saying: "Go get my robe. Go to my closet and get my robe." Now, this robe was not like a bathrobe we wear when we get out of the shower. It was a mantle. "Go get my mantle and put it on my boy's shoulders."

"Wait a minute," say the servants. "He smells like a pig."

"Doesn't matter," says the father. "He will take a bath in a minute. Ceremony has to take place first."

That robe identified the young man as a son. It was like a cape. It bore the insignia of the family, so when people saw a robe, they knew the family. It wasn't a servant's garment. It was a garment of royalty.

Next, he said: "Put a ring on his hand." It wasn't just a ring to make him feel like he had a little bling on. It was a signet ring that represented three things in the Hebrew culture:

- Identity
- Authority
- Access

The ring was engraved with the family crest and represented the identity of the family name. The ring represented authority in the name of the family, and it also represented access to everything that the estate owned. That means everyone who saw that ring on the young man's finger knew he was one with the source. He could go into town, put that ring in a wax seal, and purchase anything that he needed.

"Give him a robe, give him a ring, and give him sandals."

Why are sandals important? It's because slaves didn't wear sandals. They walked around barefooted in the dust and mud. But feet had to be washed to put on sandals. Scripture doesn't tell us this, but there was probably a foot washing that took place there. The father probably washed his son's feet just as Jesus washed the disciples' feet.

Peter said to Him, "You shall never wash my feet!"

Jesus answered him, "If I do not wash you, you have no part with Me."

John 13:8 NKJV

His father more than likely washed his feet out of custom or culture. It would have identified him as part of the family.

Now the son shifted from lack of ownership to access, and from access to ownership. When we step back into the estate, we receive authority. Authority is in the name we carry, our purpose and our assignment.

The son had abandoned all these things. He abandoned the identity, the authority and the access. But he knew he had to get back to his father's house, back to his source, to return to the family estate. So, he got up and went back and found the father waiting for him.

Then the father said:

"And bring the fatted calf here and kill it, and let us eat and be merry; for this my son was dead and is alive again; he was lost and is found." And they began to be merry.

Luke 15:23-24 NKJV

6

Mindset Matters

THE MOST IMPORTANT QUESTION WE SHOULD ASK in relation to sonship is this: What motivates us? As we examine our motives, it reveals our mindset—that of a child or a son.

Recall from Galatians 4 that the terms *slave*, *orphan*, and *child* are synonymous when discussing sonship. Even though the child is an heir—the owner of everything—he or she is no different from an slave. Remember that the evolution from child to son is a process. Uncovering our motives is an important part of that process. We discover things about ourselves. We learn to ask: "Is that thought from the mindset of a son or a child?" We need to learn this prayer: *God, what is motivating me in this area of my life?*

Christians sing songs like, *I'm the Friend of God*, and *What a Friend We Have in Jesus*. But true friendship is not well-understood in Western culture. When we become a friend, we make ourselves vulnerable. When we relate to God as our source, we make ourselves vulnerable to him, but fear can hinder the relationship. It's silly, really. Do you think there is anything about us that's going to shock God? We're not going to say something in prayer and then have God say: "Whoa, wait a minute. What did you say? You really *did* steal that candy in the third grade? Oh Greg...and all this time, I thought you were innocent."

No, we're not going to catch God by surprise. He already knows it was the Baby Ruth and not the Snickers Bar. Here's the funny thing though: he needs *us* to know that he knows. When we know that he knows that he knows that we know, then we can begin to know him even as we are known by him. (Know what I mean?)

SON OR CHILD?

Now you are no longer a slave but God's own child. And since you are his child, God has made you his heir.

Galatians 4:7 NLT

Therefore you are no longer a slave, but a son; and if a son, then an heir also <u>through God's own act.</u>

Galatians 4:7 Weymouth New Testament

Wherefore thou - Who believest in Christ. Art no more a servant - Like those who are under the law. But a son - Of mature age. And if a son, then an heir of all the promises, and of the all-sufficient God himself.

Galatians 4:7 (John Wesley's Explanatory Notes)

"Through God's own act." From the notes of John Wesley, we see that we are heirs, not just of "all the promises," but also an heir of "the all-sufficient God himself.'" He is our heritage.

The orphan (or child) spirit is not something you can cast out, because it is ungodly beliefs and/or attitudes of our flesh that have been developing over a lifetime. It has become part of our personality and character. It must be displaced (put to death) by a personal experience in the Father's love and a revelation of the spirit of sonship. This will require a re-positioning of our lives.

The spirit of sonship is all about having a heart attitude of submission—being subject to another's mission. Jesus himself said:

The Son can do nothing of Himself, unless it is something He sees the Father doing; for whatever the Father does, these things the Son also does in like manner.

John 5:19

In Hebrews 12:9, "Be subject" is also the word *submission*. In the Greek, this word means "to get underneath and to push up." So, to have the spirit of sonship is to put yourself underneath another's mission and do all that you can to make them successful, knowing that as a son/daughter, there is an inheritance that lies ahead. Sonship is about security, significance, identity, patience, basic trust, faithfulness, loyalty, humility, and being others-oriented.

Religion has schooled us in developing an orphan mindset. Until we can identify our motives as either orphan or son, we cannot become completely free of religion. Our orphan mindset must be displaced through personal experience in the Father's love and the revelation of the spirit of sonship. This will require a repositioning in our lives.

VULNERABILITY

The Father's love has been more of a mystery than reality to us in Western culture. Sure, we talk about the love of the Father, even the experience of his love, but when we encounter Father's love as a son or daughter, it wrecks us. That's because it's more than knowing God loves us. An encounter with God's love is something we step into. It undoes us and approves us at the same time. It celebrates us and corrects us. It convicts us and validates us. In the natural realm, through religion, we would not be validated by such an experience; we would be excommunicated for even talking about it.

The Father's love looks past the dark places in our lives. He sees us not as slaves, servants, or orphans, but as sons or daughters. He sees us as his very own. One of our assignments as the church is not just to be the ekklesia—not just to go out and take nations—but to bring the family back into alignment with Father's heart. He loves us so very much. He cares for us. He wants to step into our lives and let his love fix us and our situation. For this to occur, however, we have to encounter him.

Let me encourage you to pray that Father would encounter you with His love. When you sit down to pray, say:

Father, I don't know how to do this, but I know you want me to do this because I see it in your word. Father, I want to encounter you and your love. Father, come and visit me and bring me into a place that I understand your love in a greater capacity than I do right now.

Now, when we pray this, he is going to say: "I need access to all the areas of your life that you have not allowed me access to yet. I need the keys to those locked rooms because those things are holding you back from experiencing my love."

Now, you may not want to be this vulnerable with other Christians. They are not perfect; we are all in process. Sometimes, Christians put our stuff on the street. Learn to be vulnerable with God. He is your friend. You can be vulnerable with friends. Jesus told his disciples:

Greater love has no one than this: to lay down one's life for one's friends. You are my friends if you do what I command. I no longer call you servants, because a servant does not know his master's business. Instead, I have called you friends, for everything that I learned from my Father I have made known to you.

John 15:13-15 NIV

Proverbs tells us:

*A person of too many friends comes to ruin,
But there is a friend who sticks closer than a brother.*

Proverbs 18:24 NASB

Abraham and God were friends. They passed the place of a father-son relationship and moved into a friendship. The vulnerability brought them to a place of bonding that they could not have had without friendship. We are going to displace this mindset of a servant that we have in our lives. We are friends with Jesus.

SUBMISSION

Sonship requires a heart of submission. Religion is an institutionalized system of practices, ordinances, regulations and rituals we do in the hope of pleasing God. It is a pseudo-submission, as Paul told Timothy: "holding to a form of godliness although they have denied its power; avoid such people as these." (2 Timothy 3:5).

We may think, *If I come to church, God will love me more.*

We have established the fact that God never told us to *go* to church. He told us to *be* the church. So, everywhere we go, the church goes.

If I pay my tithes, God will bless me.

No, we do not tithe out of obligation; we tithe from relationship and honor. Tithing, under the Melchizedek order, is relational, not obligational. We don't have to pay our tithe. We get to pay our tithe. It's a privilege.

Tithing to get gain is the proverbial carrot on a stick. Religion hangs a carrot in front of us. It's enticing; it keeps us moving, but we never get to taste the promise. Religion makes all kinds of promises, but it can't deliver.

Relationship delivers. The Kingdom of God is based on relationship—the relationship between the Father (as our source) and his sons and daughters (his partners in the family business). The entire kingdom is based on relationship, not religion. Why is this good news? Don't relationships come and go? Wax and wane? Human relationships do. A relationship with God is different; it is rock solid. There is nothing we can do to cause God to love us any more than he already does. If there is variance, it is in our willingness to expose ourselves to God's love. Nothing in love can be forced upon us. Loves calls, invites, draws. It does not force.

Trusting in God's love gives us permission to step out in confidence. We are good! We are righteous. We cannot be any more righteous than we are right now. Why? Because righteousness is a relational gift. *Righteousness* means, "right standing or right relationship." God has given us a free gift of righteousness which puts us in right standing with him.

When we give gifts at Christmas, do people earn those gifts? No. We give a gift because we love somebody. We get gifts because somebody loves us. Sometimes gifts don't fit, so we have to re-gift them, regardless of the love they represent. God's gifts always fit. Here is the best gift.

> *For if by the offense of the one, death reigned through the one, much more will those who receive the abundance of grace and of the gift of righteousness reign in life through the One, Jesus Christ.*
>
> Romans 5:17 NASB

That is my life verse. The latter part of that verse is, "Those who receive the abundance of grace and the gift of righteousness will reign." That word reign is spelled R-E-I-G-N, not R-A-I-N. We don't get wet. We reign in life through the one Jesus Christ. Amazing!

EMPOWERED TO REIGN

Grace is not a coping mechanism that God gives us to endure difficulties in life. Grace is the empowerment to reign in life.

Paul quoted Jesus in 2 Corinthians 12:9: "My grace is sufficient for you." Religion preaches that verse, but it interprets it in a peculiar way: "His grace will enable you to cope with whatever difficult things come into your life." God was telling Paul: "I'm not removing this difficulty from your life, because my grace is sufficient for you. My grace will empower you to overcome it.

Religion says God has graced us to be able to live with the problem. Kingdom says grace will empower us to overcome it. "You have the power! You're a son of God! Take care of it, Paul." That is the definition of grace. "Those that received the abundance of grace and the gift of righteousness will rule." That word rule is *basilio*, which comes from the root *basilea*. It means, "to become king, to rule."

There is an empowerment through the abundance of grace that is released in our lives to be kings. Kings are not powerless. If one is powerless, they are not a king.

- Kings have power.
- Kings have territory.
- Kings have influence.
- Kings have dominion.

Paul told the Roman church that if they received this abundance of grace—this overwhelming and overflowing grace that can't be measured—if they allowed it to enter their lives, they would rule and reign in life. The word *receive* means, "to grab with our fist and hold on to." So, reach out and embrace it!

We are to grasp this abundance of grace—this gift of relationship and right standing with God—so we can reign in life. Not in the hereafter; not after the resurrection; not after the return of the Lord; but right here and now in this life. We have the ability—yes, and the *responsibility*—to rule and reign. We have authority in the sphere of influence God has given us.

When we step into a sphere of influence, that doesn't mean we lord over others who are there. We don't find in scripture where God's original intent was for you and me to rule *over* each other. God never wanted Israel to have a king except him. (Unfortunately, they insisted.) We are called to rule *alongside* one another. The sphere of influence that God has given you empowers the influence God has given me. What God has given me empowers what God has given you. Together, we empower one another.

When we receive this gift of righteousness, we rule in this life as kings. When things outside the kingdom invade our sphere of influence, they must submit to us.

In America, we have a limited understanding of kingdom. Why? Because we did what Adam did—we committed treason. "King

George, we're done with you. Take your tea and...um, drink it from the harbor." Yeah, right. That's what we said. "We're not going to be under the king."

John Adams said: "We'll have no king but Jesus." The preachers stood in pulpits in the mid-1700s and preached liberty and freedom from tyranny and taxes. It was the clergy that stirred up the Revolutionary War. We need preachers like that today, instead of skinny-jeans fellas teaching "Seven Ways to Be a Better You" as they strut around like banty roosters with microphones, trying to impress people with their gifts. That ain't changing nothing.

We are here to change our culture, not our hair color. Our job is to make sure the King's heart is manifested through the kingship he has given us. He is the King of kings. He is the Lord of lords. We are the little lords. It's all about the "L." Some folks look at me and say: "What the 'L' Greg?" I tell 'em: "It's all about the big 'L' and the little 'l.' You gotta get your L's right." Hallelujah.

> *They do not know nor do they understand;*
> *They walk around in darkness;*
> *All the foundations of the earth are shaken.*
> *I said, "You are gods,*
> *And all of you are sons of the Most High.*
> *Nevertheless you will die like men,*
> *And fall like one of the princes."*
>
> Psalm 82:5-7

The word *Lord* means, "those who steward the land and the finances of the king." Would you like to have more land—meaning more territory, a greater sphere of influence? Maybe more finances to advance the kingdom? Well, God wants us to have that, too.

Know the term landlord? Some of us *have* one. Some of us *are* one. I like being one better. That is where God wants us to be—one who stewards the land and finances. We are kings. John said it. Peter said it. Paul said it. Jesus is the King of kings and the Lord of lords. We are a kingdom of kings and priests. Amen.

And on His robe and on His thigh He has a name written: "KING OF KINGS, AND LORD OF LORDS."

Revelation 19:16

Relationship is defined as a significant connection between two or more things; it is the state of being related to something else, like people related by birth, adoption or marriage.

We have a royal relationship with the Father through the rebirth. We have sonship through adoption. And we have a love relationship through marriage as the Bride of Christ. Thus, our relationship with God is threefold: birth, adoption, and marriage.

> We have a royal relationship with the Father through the rebirth. We have sonship through adoption. And we have a love relationship through marriage as the Bride of Christ.

A CHILD AND A MATURE ONE

In the following pages (this chapter and the next), we'll compare a child's mindset to a son's or daughter's mindset. In this comparison, I'm using *child* as an immature person. Further, I'm drawing my comparisons based on a child who has not grown up; hence their immaturity has intensified. These are not children who are striving to grow and make mistakes along the way. These are chronically immature, childish people, held back by religion and the pseudo-spirituality it peddles as the "true gospel." In truth, there's a little bit of both in all of us—the mature and the immature. We are all sons and daughters; we are all children. Why? Because we are all growing. That's what living things do, right? They grow.

We'll start with image.

IMAGE

❖ **How does a child see God?**

A child sees God as a master. He's the big "Oh God!" up in the sky. He dwells in another realm, another dimension. God is there; I am here; and he's my master. He lords over me from afar. He's this guy with a long, white beard and a stick, ready to knock me on the head when I mess up. Many people hold to that image of God. "Jesus is coming, and man, is he pissed!"

Jonathan Edwards was a great preacher of the 18th century. In 1741, he preached a sermon that started the First Great Awakening. *Sinners in the Hands of an Angry God* was powerful, violent, even haunting. It's incredible that people still study it today. Unfortunately, it was wildly inaccurate. God is not ready to fry sinners over the fires of hell. What about sinners approaching a loving father? No, not slippery grace that lets us slide through life doing whatever our flesh wants and getting forgiveness as easy as a pack of smokes from a vending machine. I'm talking about the true, unadulterated love that exposes every dark thing and cleanses it out of our lives. It's one thing to scare the hell out of people. That's actually quite easy when they are beset with guilt. It's quite another thing to *keep* the hell out of people. (That takes a bit more besetting.)

> *I now rejoice, not that you were made sorrowful, but that you were made sorrowful to the point of repentance; for you were made sorrowful according to the will of God, so that you might not suffer loss in anything through us. For the sorrow that is according to the will of God produces a repentance without regret, leading to salvation, but the sorrow of the world produces death.*
>
> 2 Corinthians 7:9-10

A child sees a Jonathan Edwards-type of God. Tragically, she misses the God whose love brings us into our true identity—who he called us to be.

❖ How Does a Son See God?

Sons and daughters see God as a loving father.

- He loves us in spite of ourselves.
- He loves us when we are good, and he loves us when we are bad.
- He loves us when we are right, and he loves us when we are wrong.
- He loves us when we do things that bring life, and he loves us when we do things that bring death.
- He never stops loving us.

God sees a beauty in us that we often don't see.

- Where we see muddy feet, he sees feet that will carry us to spread the gospel.
- Where we see confusion, he sees a pioneering spirit that isn't afraid to charge into the unknown.
- Where we see sorrow, he sees a heart tender enough to feel the pain of others.

Each of us is the creation of a loving, beautiful, all-powerful God. That is the essence of who we are. The junk in our lives? That's what we're working on. But never, ever, ever lose sight of the end goal: the glory of God in the highest, and on earth, peace and goodwill to all mankind.

Sometimes, the process of refinement takes a turn that we don't understand. I was raised with a mom and dad who loved me. I knew my parents loved me no matter what. And trust me, I tested that love many times. I actually got quite good at proving that love, if I do say so myself.

My daddy tried to scare me a few times. "Boy, I will kill you and make another one just like you."

In my child's mindset, I thought, "Uh oh, I did it now. He's got 40 acres out back and a shovel in the barn. They won't find me 'til spring."

But Daddy wasn't telling me he didn't love me. He was scolding me, and occasionally, he backed it up. Well...I was the one backing up. He was the one with the switch in his hand. (I guess that's why God put padding back there.)

Yep, I heard: "Greg, this is going to hurt me more than it is going to hurt you." And I'd think: *Yeah, you're a liar. There's no way in the world is it going to hurt you more.*

Many years later, I had to give my son a spanking for the first time. It was gentle, but it broke my heart. I sent him out of the room to his mom, and I cried long after his tears dried up. (Heck, he got a cookie and a glass of milk out of the deal. All I got was a scowl.)

The last time I got a whipping, I was probably 15 or 16. I had disrespected my mother and was fortunate to have survived. My daddy gave me a whipping like I had never had. My life flashed before my eyes. Yet I could hear him crying as he administered justice. It broke his heart. For the first time after a whipping, he pulled me into his arms and hugged me. That really wasn't in his makeup to do that. But it so impacted him, what he had to do, that it changed him and me. That was an expression of his love to me.

> The difference between a child and a son is this: the child fears the whip, but the son fears the heart.

It was a traumatic event, but I didn't leave that experience thinking my daddy hated me. I knew he loved me, and that messed with me more than the whipping. From that moment on, there was nothing he could do to me physically. It was the thought of hurting that man's heart that haunted me. My dad was a loving father. Our heavenly Father is a loving father. Sometimes he will take us to the woodshed. Be quick to repent. Be quick to come clean with the things that he is asking us about, so we can avoid the woodshed.

While Jonathan Edwards understood the wrath of God, he didn't understand the love of God. The difference between a child and a son is this: the child fears the whip, but the son fears the heart. It's one thing to get punished, but, when breaking God's heart means more than a scalded backside, we will know true maturity.

That comes in handy as parents the day junior stands up and we see six-foot, two-inches of lean muscle staring down at us. If love isn't in those eyes by then, we're in for a long day.

RELATIONSHIP

❖ **How does a child see his relationship to God?**

A child feels like a servant. They do things out of obligation to God. *If I don't do this, God's going to punish me. I have to work to earn my place in the kingdom.*

> As in life, so with God: Love comes before conception. At least...it should.

This is a transactional mentality. And it works...sort of. See, God will respond to any heart that is turned to him, regardless of what it looks like on the outside. There are people who cannot articulate God the way some do in a Judea-Christian culture. But they are reaching out with what they have. The issue is that they are severely limited in what they can receive from God. As a loving Father, he won't give us more than we can handle. Strange as it seems, the unrestrained blessings of God would kill us. Give a daughter the keys to the tractor, and she'll head to the field to plow and plant. Give a child the keys, and he'll drive it straight through the side of the barn, laughing and yelling "Yee hah!"

Our true, deep relationship with God is not based on what we do. As mature ones, we operate out of relationship with the Father. Relationship is not transactional. We don't do the things in order to have a relationship with the Father. We do things *as a result* of relationship with the Father. As in life, so with God: Love comes before conception. At least...it should.

❖ How does a son see his relationship with God?

A mature son or daughter feels like a member of the family. What does that mean? It means having access to everything our mother and father have; it's all there for us.

As a boy, I'd sit at Mom's table as she put food out. My mother didn't have a large menu, but she did well with what she had. One day, she pulled everything out of the refrigerator, filled a big pot, and told us it was goulash. ("You see, Greg, *goulash* is a Greek word meaning 'full, lots of stuff.' It also means 'to dump the contents of the kitchen.' It's rooted in the word *stew-eous*, meaning 'to stir and stir until it looks like something edible. LOL!'")

We kids devoured it.

It's all in how we define it, I guess. Strange as it may seem, I ate at Mom's table all my young life, and you know what? She never charged me; not one red cent! Today, as a grown man (who has obviously made up for the limited menu of his youth), I can walk into my mother's house, go to the refrigerator, pull out anything I want, sit down at her table and start eating. If she walked in on me, she'd say: "Greg, Son, do you want anything else?"

Why can I do that? Because I can't afford to feed myself? No! It's because I'm her son. I still have access to things she has. You know what else? I'm more likely to walk into that house with a bag of groceries and fill that refrigerator, because I am no longer a child. And I promise you, if we're ever down to our last meal together, she's getting mine. You feeling me? That's sonship. That's family. That's love. That's just the way it is.

It's the same with our heavenly Father. Everything that Daddy has, we have access to it. He's already given it to us through Jesus. We are here to give it forward; sons and daughters of God, bringing the kingdom to a hungry world.

INTERDEPENDENCY

❖ **How does a child see interdependency?**

A child sees himself as self-reliant and independent. Consequently, he sees interdependency with others as a threat to his self-reliance. He prides himself as being a maverick. He doesn't need anyone, and no one needs him. "That's just the way I like it!" In reality, this is abject loneliness disguised as strength. It's crying out for more while being limited by the self-imposed inability to count beyond the number one. It's pride hiding a festering wound. Tragically of all, when we wall out others, that wall also repels God.

❖ **How does the son see interdependency?**

Sons are interdependent and acknowledge their need for God. The world—especially Western culture—says we are to be self-made men and women; to be someone who doesn't need anybody; don't depend on other people for things. Well, we depend on God like a fish depends on water. He is our source. We must be interdependent on him, and we must be willing to acknowledge that need.

Woe to the one who quarrels with his Maker—

A piece of pottery among the other earthenware pottery pieces!

Will the clay say to the potter, "What are you doing?"

Or the thing you are making say, "He has no hands"?

Isaiah 45:9

PROBLEM SOLVING

❖ **How does a child solve problems?**

A child mentality is an escape mentality. He is always looking for a way out, some means to escape his problems. "Any opportunity I get, I'm outta here. Goodbye, cruel world. Don't forget to email once in a while."

Religion is the same way. It puts more focus on heaven than on earth. Why? Because religion knows it cannot dominate heaven, so it attempts to dominate earth. However, religion cannot dominate earth if there are sons and daughters who have a clear understanding of their true calling: to rule and reign on the earth.

❖ How does a son solve problems?

A son is always looking for a way to solve a problem, but a child is looking to avoid and escape a problem. That's why religion is more focused on leaving earth than staying and restoring earth. Rather than occupying earth, religion looks for a ticket out of here and the promise of not returning until the conflict is resolved.

Now, don't get me wrong. I believe the Lord is returning. In fact, I'm looking forward to it. (Truth be told, some people are also looking forward to my departure, but...that's another story.) Yet I realize there is work to be done before Jesus arrives. See, religion teaches a rescue mentality—we are being raptured out of this wicked ole' earth. Kingdom sees it differently. Jesus is coming for a mature bride. We are part of that maturation process. For that reason, I really don't expect him to come today or next week. Why? Because I have family that are not saved. I have friends who are not born again. I want to see them in the Kingdom of God. I want to see them living out their purpose.

> If these are the last days, let them be the last days for stupid theology.

Religious people, in their escapism mentality, pray: "Lord, get us out of here today." Anytime something goes wrong in our country, our culture or our society, religion declares: "These are the end times. These are the last days. Jesus said these things would happen. He's gotta be coming back any minute now. Cash in your kid's college fund and max out your credit cards! Jesus'll be here any day now!"

Twenty years later, these are still the last days. Meanwhile, your kid had to go to college on student loans and Visa cancelled all your cards. If these are the last days, let them be the last days for stupid theology.

In 1988, a book came out: *88 Reasons Why the Rapture Will Be in 1988*. The information was false, obviously, but I didn't know it at the time. See, my books hadn't come out yet, so I didn't know any better. So, worried about my loved ones going to hell, I jumped in my pickup and drove like a man on fire from Dallas, Texas to Amory, Mississippi. I had to make sure my family was really born again, because Jesus was coming in a few months. Actually, it was September of 1988. He was supposed to show up any minute.

Well, they assured me they were all saved, so with them all okay, I drove back, expecting the truck to veer off the road at any moment. I was confident in my heart that this was the last year of my time on earth. I would soon be leaving Texas and going to heaven. (Although a lot of Texans would argue the order of those events.) I knew I'd meet my family in the air.

Well, of all the bad luck! January 1, 1989, rolled around and nothing had happened. Like any enterprising theologian, the author wrote: *89 Reasons Why Jesus is Coming in 1989*, or something to that effect. "We missed the year by one, so it's 89 reasons, not 88 reasons." I thought, *Oh, my Lord, I am not making another trip back to Mississippi. No way that old Chevy will make it that far.*

Next thing I knew, January 01, 1990 rolled around and still nothing happened. The author then came out with more predictions: 1993, and then 1994. By the time he got to 1997, nobody was listening. At least...not to him.

Why is the church so gullible with that kind of thinking? Again, I am not denying the fact that Jesus is returning. But the Bible says: "But about that day and hour no one knows, not even the angels of heaven, nor the Son, but the Father alone" (Matthew 24:36). Jesus said there will be a few signs, but we have misinterpreted these signs massively.

Recently, a fella from San Antonio wrote a book about blood moons. He posits that this is the sign that Jesus is coming soon. *The* moon is turning to blood. All these things are happening. *Buy my book; buy my book; buy my book.* Well, the blood moons came and went. Those books are about 50% off now, I think. The rapture never happened. Guess I'll unpack my suitcase.

When are we going to stop buying into that...baloney? When are we going to get off of the bandwagon that everything bad that happens is a sign of the end times? We need to deal with the bad things, not whip up the hysteria of false hope with assurances of escaping this veil of tears.

We need to get on with occupying instead of trying to exit the planet. Don't fear the world. Jesus was not afraid of the world. The Bible calls him a friend of sinners. We need to be a friend of sinners. Religion says to separate ourselves from those of the world. It wants us to huddle in our church buildings and sing songs about the imminent return of our Savior. Yet the Bible says we have him in our lives already.

> *Jesus answered and said to him, "If anyone loves Me, he will follow My word; and My Father will love him, and We will come to him and make Our dwelling with him.*
>
> John 14:23

Why are we looking for the arrival of someone who is already here? Jesus said to go out among the world, be a friend to sinners, and share the gospel. He would not have said that if he were not with us.

APPROVAL

❖ **How does the child see approval or affirmation?**

A child strives for praise, approval, and acceptance from people. We all know people like that—people who crave recognition. *Did I do good? Did you see what I did? Am I great or what?* Every time we tell a story, they try to tell a better one. They compete for the limelight. We give a testimony. They have a better one. They need to be heard. It brings affirmation to their life. Their testimony is always more dramatic. They have lived through more trauma or hardship than we have. They bring more miracles, signs, wonders, and prophetic words than we do. We are number two to their number "me."

This is a child mentality, an orphan mindset. We must grow out of this. We have all been there—and who doesn't like to hear "good job!"—but it is something we do not want to grow dependent upon. When we hear somebody give a testimony or tell a story, don't follow with, "Let me tell you this one." Truly rejoice with them in what they are sharing and all that God is doing in their life. The time will come for you to share your testimony. Be patient and mindful of the Lord's timing.

When we find ourselves around others who are more esteemed than we are, don't talk, listen. God has most likely brought us to this group to learn from their experience. Chances are, you are there to learn. It's hard to listen with your mouth open...so listen well!

When God opens new doors for me to be in the presence of others, I don't come in saying: "Hey, I'm apostle Dr. Greg Hood. How are you guys doing?" No, I say: "Hey, I'm Greg. That's 'Greg' with one 'g.' My parents couldn't afford two. How're y'all?" Then I listen to what they have to say. I do not engage in the conversation. I know better than to do that. I'm there to learn, not there to give. Sometimes, it's better to receive than to give.

When you sit down to dine with a ruler,
Consider carefully what is before you,
And put a knife to your throat
If you are a person of great appetite.

Proverbs 23:1-2

❖ **How does the son see approval or affirmation?**

A son knows he is totally accepted by God's love and justified by his grace. My affirmation—my approval as a son—comes from God's love and understanding. I am justified by his grace. We don't need people to pat us on the back, even though that is good sometimes.

(Especially if we're choking on a peach pit.) Let acknowledgment come voluntarily. Don't go around begging others for feedback unless you are in training. People who look for a response are usually feeding a faltering self-image and expecting praise to shore it up. Criticism will destroy them, so they attempt to forestall it.

"How was my message, brother? Was it good? Great? Did the angels weep? An' the dead rise? Did you hear Jesus say: "Darn! That boy can preach up a storm! I betcha did. Huh? Huh??"

"Well, you misquoted three scriptures, and your doctrine was way off. You were also a tad long-winded. Four hours is a long time for anyone's bladder. If you cut it back a bit, people might not snore so loudly. Oh, and it might help if you brushed your teeth before calling people up for prayer. Your breath could knock a buzzard off a dung pile."

People craving approval don't want to hear that kind of feedback. All they want to hear is: "That was the best message I have ever heard, preacher. I believe you could get the devil saved."

Or if the person is in business and she lands a moderate sale, the daughter will let her success do the talking. The child, on the other hand, will pump the boss for accolades.

"Hey Boss. See what I did? Eh? Was that great or what? Our bottom line's gonna be off the charts this year. I bet I'll get an amazing bonus? What'ya say, Boss?"

"Well, Elena, I'm happy you're finally doing your job."

A son wants criticism. They are students of the craft—whatever their craft is. They cultivate choice relationships with trusted friends and advisors. They know who they are seeking feedback from, and they value their opinions.

A son is not looking for high praise when he does something well. He is fine with a handshake, even in a business deal. We should be able to do things for people without heaps of praise or volumes of compliments. That's what horses, cowboy hats, guitars and sunsets are for. *All in a day's work, ma'am. I'll be seeing ya'.*

Soliciting feedback when we really want compliments is like asking people to lie to us—something that most people will readily do. Let's face it: nobody likes conflict. They'll pick up your vibe and feed you what they think you are fishing for. In the end, the exchange corrupts both parties.

The most reliable feedback is from God. He alone defines us. But be ready. He doesn't pull any punches.

MINISTRY

Now, when we say ministry in Western culture, we think of preaching, pastoring, pulpits on Sunday morning and offering plates. But that's not it.

People often ask me: "When did you go into full-time ministry?"

"Well, when I got born again."

"You mean you have been in full-time ministry since the day you were born again?"

"Yep. I've installed vinyl siding on houses. I drove a truck for a while. I painted houses, played music, even preached a lick or two."

See, people don't think that's full-time ministry, but it is. Life is full-time ministry. The key is understanding that *ministry* means "service."

The United States uses terms like the Department of State, the Department of Health, the Department of Defense, the Department of the Military. But in countries that are kingdom-minded, like Great Britain, they use terms like the Ministry of Defense, the Ministry of State, the Ministry of Education. They use the word *ministry* in its correct capacity, which is service.

❖ How does a child see ministry?

A child has a need for personal achievement in ministry. They seek to impress God and others. They have no motive to serve. Some people in professional ministry go to seminary, develop a skill for public speaking, and expect an easy job and good money. They plan to golf on Monday and Friday, visit the sick on Wednesday, take off on Tuesday, and do a business meeting on Thursday. Saturday is for hunting and fishing (and college football, of course). Sunday, they have to put up with the rabble in rags begging for crumbs that fall from the plate, but at least it pays the bills.

They are advancement minded. *I could get into this little church, then I could get to a bigger church, and then on to an even bigger church.* They approach it like a business. *I can make this business work, then I'll add this business and another business. Maybe I'll sell this one and buy another, or start a new business.*

They have personal goals. They want to achieve things in life to impress God and other people. That is a child mentality.

❖ How does a son see ministry?

A son's service is motivated by deep gratitude for being unconditionally loved and accepted by God.

For example, I am teaching this subject not to impress you. As a matter of fact, as a redneck, I struggle to impress anybody, even my wife. She loves me in spite of me.

Joan and I get about four or five days a month home. We are usually on the road, flying, going to places that have twenty people or several thousand people. I don't mind small gatherings. Sometimes the bigger gatherings are bigger headaches. We go where we go, and we do what we do because we have a deep gratitude towards the Father for unconditionally loving us and accepting us into his family.

That is why we serve; that is why we minister.

That needs to be our motivation in all we do in life, whether it is taking care of our children, our grandchildren, cooking, cleaning, running a business or changing the oil in the church bus. If we are in arts and entertainment, it's our motive for doing concerts and shows. If we are in media, it's our motive for doing our newscast and writing articles and podcasts. Whatever it may be, we don't do it to grab status. Our service should be because God loves us unconditionally and we know it.

When I think about it that way, I can do anything. I can go into places I don't want to go. I can eat food I don't want to eat. Heck, with that attitude, I could probably even pastor people. (*Oh, God, don't put me through more than I can endure.*)

I told God one time, "Lord, if I could just pastor without the people, I would really like that." The next week, half the church left. God said: "How's that, Greg?"

Seriously, pastoring is not my gift. I love teaching. Yes, my feet hurt from standing so long. I get tired from traveling. I stay up late working on my books. But I love it because I know God loves me and I have the privilege of ministering to his people.

That is the motivation of a son and daughter.

FUTURE

❖ **How does a child see their future?**

> An orphan mentality says: You gotta fight like you're the third monkey on the ramp to Noah's Ark, and brother, it's starting to rain.

When it comes to their future, a child fights for everything they can get. A child mentality is a crab mentality. Ever see a bucket of crabs? One crab gets almost to the top, ready to crawl out, and another crab reaches up and pulls him down to get ahead of him. That is a child mentality. *I need to crawl over you for me to get out.* Some people in the business world call it "the corporate ladder." *I have to do everything I can do to get up this ladder ahead of everybody else. If I can't get ahead of them, then I will never get ahead.*

An orphan mentality says: You gotta fight like you're the third monkey on the ramp to Noah's Ark, and brother, it's starting to rain.

❖ How does a son see his future?

Sonship releases inheritance to the son or daughter. His attitude is: "If the Father wants me at another level in this company, he'll make a way for me. My gift will make room for me in that place. If God wants me to climb a ladder, he will give me a ladder. I don't have to pull my fellow crabs back down into the bucket. God will make a way for me to get promoted out of this crab bucket!"

> *A person's gift makes room for him*
> *And brings him before great people.*
>
> Proverbs 18:16

If we are being faithful with the little, God calls us to be a master over much.

> *His master replied, "Well done, good and faithful servant! You have been faithful with a few things; I will put you in charge of many things. Come and share your master's happiness!"*
>
> Matthew 25:23 NIV

Kings will look at you and say: That's the one I want to promote in my realm.

> *For not from the east, nor from the west,*
> *Nor from the desert comes exaltation;*
> *But God is the Judge;*
> *He puts down one and exalts another.*
>
> Psalm 75:6-7

Daniel was promoted above all the wise men of his day because he heard from God and did not buy into the deception that others were doing. He didn't use their deception as a method of advancement. He called on the God of his fathers. He was faithful with what God gave him, and God promoted him.

It worked out pretty well for him, but later he had to go through the lions' den. Many Christians think, *God, why have you put me in here to fend off these cats? Please don't eat me. Eat the other guy!* Daniel didn't do that. He thought: *I'll be fine. You should worry about your cats; they're hungry. And I am not the blue-plate special today.*

It does not matter if we are in the lions' den all our life. If God led us there, good will come from it. We don't have to make the best of it. The best will come out of it. Our inheritance provides for our future.

SELF-IMAGE

- ❖ **How does a child see himself?**

A child's self-image is shame-based; it's fueled by self-rejection that comes from comparing himself to others. People who live in shame need that broken off them. Deliverance is one way to do it, but another way is to grow out of it.

- ❖ **How does a son see himself?**

A son or daughter's self-image comes from a positive perspective. It is affirmed because they know how much God loves them and values them. It is very important that we understand our worth. The most valuable thing heaven had was spent to get us back into the family—the blood of the Son.

Don't compare yourself to others, because others have different assignments than you do, even if you are doing the same thing. Don't judge yourself by the success of others. That is not sonship. Don't reject yourself because it looks like somebody is getting ahead of you. The scripture says for you and me to prefer our brothers and sisters above ourselves.

Do nothing from selfishness or empty conceit, but with humility consider one another as more important than yourselves.

Philippians 2:3 NASB

CORRECTION

❖ **How does a child respond to correction?**

A child has difficulty receiving correction. They must be right. They easily get their feelings hurt and will close themselves off to others. If someone in leadership corrects them, they may leave the group thinking: *Who does she think she is, correcting me? She doesn't appreciate my gift. She doesn't appreciate my contribution to this congregation or what I do. I am leaving and going somewhere where they'll appreciate me.*

When that happens, you know you are dealing with a child mentality.

❖ **How does a son respond to correction?**

A son sees gracious correction as encouragement; it's a blessing and a need in their lives. They want their faults exposed and put to death. A son thinks: *this leader saw something in me that is a fault and possibly a snare in my life. I am grateful for that. Now I can put that thing to death and dispose of it out of my life.*

If it is something life-controlling, we might even need some deliverance.

How we respond to correction—in church, in our workplace, in the home—is important. People have left congregations because they were corrected and got offended. Instead of making a life change, they left because they did not want their personal issues to be exposed.

Mindset Matters

How we deal with correction on our job or in our business makes a big difference. We can tell our supervisor: "Who do you think you are correcting me? I know what I'm doing."

He'll say, "Go punch your timecard, and we will mail you a check. You're outta here."

In church, people act differently. They will start a coup. They will find the most troublesome person in the church and whisper: "Do you know what Pastor did? We need to get the elders together and vote on him again."

Sons see correction as grace in our lives to expose faults so we can grow unto life. Hallelujah.

7

Child to Son

IN THIS FINAL CHAPTER, we will continue our comparison of children to sonship, citing how immature ones become mature sons and daughters.

COMFORT

❖ **How does a child seek comfort?**

A child seeks comfort in counterfeit affections such as addictions, compulsions, hyper-religiosity and overwork.

People often seek comfort when things are not going their way. When all hell is breaking loose in their life, they tend to fall back into addictions. That's an orphan mentality.

It's like stressing a board that already has cracks throughout. You don't notice the cracks until pressure is applied; that's when you see the fault lines. Now, we all have faults. This is one reason God tests and tries us. He's looking for our faults, and he wants to reveal them to us. Why? To humiliate us? Of course not. Remember, this is the God who sees you in the shower. He wants to remove the faults; he wants to continue his work of salvation (restoration) in your life; he wants to make you better and better.

Not all addictions and compulsions are nefarious. While there's illegal drug use and alcoholism, other addictions appear normal, benign, even holy.

Some people resort to burning the card. What's that mean? You take a credit card and slide it so fast through that machine, it catches on fire. *Whoosh!* Off they go into compulsive shopping.

Other people throw themselves into over-work. They'll clean the house for hours until wear spots appear on the furniture, or they'll spend 20 hours a day at the office, or they'll take every available hour of overtime at the shop.

Over-eating is a big one. People embark on a see-food diet until they have to be rescued. The only way to get them out of the house is to grease the door jamb and hold up a Twinkie.

Other people resort to long hours of prayer and fasting. Now...nothing wrong with prayer and fasting. I'm describing cases where the motive is not pure. Many people tap into a false spirituality, one that feeds them what they want instead of what they need. The problem is: a false spirituality is still spiritual. The question then becomes: what spirit? People who enter the spiritual realm with intentions that are other than Holy Spirit-led can find themselves in far worse shape.

Some folks embrace hyper-religiosity for comfort. We see this every Sunday in churches across America, especially in Spirit-filled churches like Pentecostal, Charismatic, or Word of Faith churches. Their reasoning goes like this:

If I could just get to church,

If I could just hear a good message,

If I could just shout for a little bit,

If I could dance in the spirit for a minute,

If I could just run around the sanctuary...

...I'd be okay.

We shouldn't have to get to church to find comfort. We shouldn't have to huck-a-buck in the isles and ride the ceiling fans. If that's where we find our comfort, then that is a child mentality.

❖ How does a son seek comfort?

A son seeks times of quietness and solitude to rest in the father's presence and love.

As sons, we live in comfort, but that doesn't mean things don't get uncomfortable. We learn to find comfort in the midst of upheaval. We seek times of quietness and solitude to rest in the Father's presence. We need time alone to enter that place where we spend time with the Father. We talk to him. We listen to him. We just sit there and soak in his presence. It is good.

We need to learn to embrace quietness with the Father and let his presence refill us. I like those times. I can be in a room full of people chattering on about their plans for a non-existent future, and I still have a quiet time with the Lord. They can be carrying on about their CNN-informed opinions on world events, and I just sit there in peace. I have learned to draw from my quiet space with the Lord. Sons can create that clean, well-lighted space where the noise of the world dissolves like atoms falling from the air.

A son seeks this place but does not dwell there forever. It is a place to recharge, to be intimate with God, to reveal things we've been holding inside, to hear God or not hear God. That is a good place. Just knowing he is in the room yields comfort and strength.

Most of the time, God will give us what we need without us having to fast, pray, whip ourselves into a frenzy or bang our heads against the wall. Just sit in his presence. Draw from the quietness that the Father wants to deposit into your life. Hang out there for a minute, an hour, or a day.

Then get up and go back to work.

PEER RELATIONSHIPS

❖ **How does a child see peer relationships?**

A child or an orphan mentality views relationships as transactional. Peer relationships are judged according to how they will serve the child. Consequently, a child's life is embroiled in competition, rivalry and jealousy toward other's success and position.

What can you do for me if I let you have a relationship with me? I don't have time to take your call today, because you have not done things for me lately. You are a burden on me. Sure, you just need someone to listen to you, but what's in it for me?

It's friendship at a cost. Of course, that never happens in the church, right?

According to a child or an orphan mentality, relationships are based on transactions and competition. *I am better than you. I have to be better than you. I need to work harder to be better than you. You are achieving something I can't achieve. Therefore, I need something that looks better.*

That is a child mentality. Just because we see a promise of God fulfilled in someone else's life, it doesn't mean we are not going to get ours. Just because God blesses someone else, it doesn't mean he will run out of blessings for us.

The Bible tells us what to do when we see someone blessed. "Rejoice with those who rejoice, and weep with those who weep" (Romans 12:15). Yet a child will say: "Well, I don't know why God gave them that. I am a better Christian than they are. Why didn't I get what I was asking for? I pray more than she does. Look at that fat fella. Clearly, I fast more than he does. That guy lives on cheeseburgers and bacon. Heck, his driver's license picture is an aerial photo! Come on!

"And that woman on the stage...? Why do they let her sing? She can't carry a tune in a bucket. Why is she leading the Worship Team? When she opens her mouth, the angels shudder. I know she has a beautiful voice, but she destroys it getting it out."

Child to Son

The fact is, a good worship leader is not interested in people's musical gifts. She's interested in their hearts. She would rather have people occasionally miss a note than to have somebody classically trained but abysmally anointed. Why? Because it is about the heart; it is not about the gift.

A child mentality makes it about the gift. It's competition, rivalry. *What can I do to pull her down and boost me up there? I wish they wouldn't let her sing. Why don't they turn her mic down? Bless her heart.*

Jealousy, success, position; it rages on.

If I could just get Pastor to agree to let me preach, I feel like I'd have a level of success. My relationships with my peers would be better because I'd be ahead of them. Glory to God!

❖ **How does a son see peer relationships?**

A sonship mentality seeks pure relationships; he or she values humility, unity and oneness. As we value others, we are genuinely able to rejoice in their blessing and success. We may be the more accomplished singer. We may have awards on our mantle. We may post accolades on Facebook and Instagram. But when God uses someone else to hit the high notes, go to them and say: "I'm proud of you. That was awesome today. You did a good job. I am glad God is opening doors for you. Heck, the dogs outside didn't howl once!"

Let them know you want the best for them. Cheer them on. Support them. Take the humble road. Humility is not based on unworthiness. Humility finds its peace and affirmation in the unconditional love of the Father.

> *Greater love has no one than this, that a person will lay down his life for his friends.*
>
> John 15:13

Now, that word *life* doesn't mean we are going to jump in front of a bus for somebody. (Well, maybe a parked bus.) It means, "no greater love has anyone than to lay down their visions, dreams, and desires to help someone else accomplish theirs." We learn to put others first.

Interestingly, while we are helping someone else rise, God is pulling us up as well. When we prefer others, we value them. To value someone doesn't mean they have to do something our way. God only created one of you. (Praise God!) He only made one of me. (Thank you, Lord!) And there's only one of everybody else. (1,2,3,4...∞)

Let's celebrate everyone as mature sons and daughters.

Authority

- #### A Childs View of Authority

Some people see authority as a source of pain; hence they are distrustful toward those in authority, resulting in a genuine lack of heartfelt submission. Yet authority is important in our lives. In Matthew 8, a centurion came to Jesus saying: "I have a sick servant. Would you heal him?"

Jesus said: "Sure, let's go."

The centurion said: "No need to come to my house. I have been watching you, Jesus. I, like you, am a man under authority. If Caesar tells me to come, I come. If I tell one of my men to go, he goes. We operate the same way. All you have to do is speak the word, and I know my servant will be healed."

I often ask people: "Who are you aligned with? Who is the apostolic voice in your life?" If they say: "Just me and Jesus," I really don't want anything to do with them. Why? Because of their child mentality. We need authority in our life. We need people we answer to, people who will knock on our locked door once in a while.

I fear no evil, for You are with me;
Your rod and Your staff, they comfort me.

Psalm 23:4

Child to Son

Authority is good. Just as we need policemen in our community, we need spiritual authority in our lives. We need fivefold ministers to help grow us, guide us, and manage us in the things that God has called us to do and be. Many people have been hurt by the church. Well...who hasn't been hurt by the church? There is a support group for that; it is called prayer. You and the Father get alone together. He takes care of the hurt. You need to let God deal with those things in your life.

We cannot live life out of our pain. Disappointment can be healed. Accept the healing and move on.

- ❖ **A Sons view of authority.**

Sons are respectful and honoring of authority. Sons see authority as ministers for good in their life. Yes, there are those that are in positions of authority that have no business being authoritative in any capacity. Even in the pulpit, there are some crazy, evil men and women who are using that position for nefarious aims. (Did I say *evil* out loud? Oh dear.... At least I didn't say *nefarious*.) But there they are: spiritual leaders that will use us, hurt us, try to destroy us. And not just in ministry: bosses, husbands, wives, children, politicians, Dodge trucks, bad hair weaves—all will disappoint us at some point. All authority structures will fail at times. Nothing's perfect! Get used to it. And understand that God puts authority in our lives for our good. Seek the hand of God in all things, and be respectful.

Now, if they're abusing you, or if they're doing things that are unlawful, illegal, or toxic, you absolutely need to get away from them. Also, report them to higher authorities if that's an option. But don't avoid authority for the rest of your life. Find a job, a marriage, a church, or a leader that leads to life. Let Holy Spirit lead you into a safe place where authority can be trusted to bring good into your life.

SIN

❖ **How does a child handle other people's sin?**

A child mindset uses accusations and exposure to make themselves look good and others look bad. This is huge. How we handle other's sin determines how our sin will be handled. If we are gracious, loving and restoring, the same can come back into our lives. On the other hand, there are people who will find somebody in sin and broadcast it to the world. That is illegal in the community that we call the Kingdom of God, and it has a way of coming back to you in spades.

> *Do not be deceived, God is not mocked; for whatever a person sows, this he will also reap.*
>
> Galatians 6:7

❖ **How a son handles other's sin?**

A son's love covers and restores others in the spirit of grace, truth and gentleness.

> *If a man be overtaken in a fault, ye which are spiritual, restore such a one in the spirit of meekness.*
>
> Galatians 6:1 KJV

Sadly, this is not always followed. The army of God tends to shoot their own wounded. We need to restore them. Everything God does is redemptive. That's what forgiveness is about...even for the "big" sins. So, someone committed adultery? Yeah? Well, the Bible says that if we are even looking at another person in lust, then we have done the same thing in our hearts. Don't condemn the sinner; restore them. Then go home and have a look at your own browsing history.

> *You hypocrite, first take the log out of your own eye, and then you will see clearly to take the speck out of your brother's eye.*
>
> Matthew 7:5 NASB

That's the thing about this kingdom: we don't get to throw many spears, but we sure want to.

Well, they have no business being in this capacity if they are doing that kind of sin.

Maybe not. But have compassion. Maybe they are struggling with things that have been in their family for years. Maybe it's an inequity of some kind. Maybe it is a curse. Maybe it is a demon, and they need a Holy Spirit-filled person to help them get delivered.

Now if our brother sins, go and show him his fault in private; if he listens to you, you have gained your brother. But if he does not listen to you, take one or two more with you, so that ON THE TESTIMONY OF TWO OR THREE WITNESSES EVERY MATTER MAY BE CONFIRMED. *And if he refuses to listen to them, tell it to the church; and if he refuses to listen even to the church, he is to be to you as a Gentile and a tax collector.*

Matthew 18:15-17 NASB

Scripture tells us that when we see a fault, we are to go to the sinning person by ourselves...without getting counseling involved, without getting on the phone to everyone we know. In Hawaii, we called it the "coconut wireless" because we get on the phone, and in the false notion of requesting prayer, we tell all about "brother so-and-so is having problems with this-and-that." We believe that we are not gossiping, praise the Lord, because it is a matter of prayer. In reality, all we did was gossip. We didn't even pray before we got on the phone.

The Bible says for us to go to him (or her) individually. Don't go angrily. Go with a heart of restoration and meekness. Why? Because if we go any other way, we could be caught in the same sin. We are dealing with spiritual dynamics. Confronting a person while we are in the flesh leaves the door open for us to receive the same invasion. Here are the biblical steps:

1. We are to sit with him and talk about the thing we have observed and offer to help bring restoration. Make the commitment to meet with him, pray and minister to him for restoration.

2. If he won't receive that, go and find another person, one that is trustworthy, and the two of you go to him.

3. If he refuses your help, go to the elders.

4. If the elders can't help him, then the elders are to bring him before the church. Its officially out of your hands at this point.

That can work if followed. The problem is, most people start with number four and work backwards.

Now, once sin has been dealt with and the sinner restored, forget it. God took our sin, and he not only forgives them, he forgets them. We need to do the same thing. We need to help people navigate through the struggles of life, and when they are restored, don't hold it against them. Don't say, "Remember ten years ago when we caught you doing <insert name of awful, terrible deed here>."

It doesn't work with our spouses. If we ask for forgiveness, and our husband or wife forgives us, we are to be like Jesus. Forget it. Don't be like the wife who lost her temper one day and resurrected everything the poor husband ever did wrong. *First she got hysterical, then she got historical.* No lasting good ever comes from a long memory.

CHRISTIAN DISCIPLINE

❖ **How does a child practice Christian discipline?**

What are Christian disciplines? Praying, fasting, doing good, helping people. A child sees these as a duty to earn God's favor. The child has no other motivation. They're not interested in truly helping others. They are driven by their own craven fear, guilt, and suspicion. Christian disciplines to a child are a means to keep up the façade.

Child to Son

- ❖ **How does a son practice Christian discipline?**

A son sees Christine disciplines as a pleasure and a delight. That's not to say that every moment is enjoyable. Rather, a son sees the deeper intent to these disciplines, and so he practices them with an eye toward the greater good.

PURITY

- ❖ **How does a child view holiness?**

A child's mentality is: *I must be holy to have God's favor.*

That viewpoint feeds our shame and guilt when we put the word *must* in the sentence. It makes it an obligation. "I *must* be holy. I *must* be pure. I *must* be circumspect. If I don't do these things, then shame and guilt increase in my life...and I deserve it!"

Folks, holiness is not a matter of what we are separated from. Just because we don't drink, smoke, dip, chew or date girls that do, it doesn't mean that we are holy. Holiness is not about being separated from something. Holiness means we are separated *unto* someone. It is akin to what Holy Spirit said in Acts 13:2.

> *While they were serving the Lord and fasting, the Holy Spirit said, "Set Barnabas and Saul apart for Me for the work to which I have called them."*

Holiness is not based on what we don't do. It's based on who we are separated unto. Holiness is based on our Father, not our actions. To think otherwise only increases unholiness in our lives.

The good news is, God is not going to guilt us into anything. He will convict us, but he will not guilt us. He will not put shame on us to bring us into a right place. He can bring correction into our lives—and he frequently does, as part of the ongoing work of salvation—but lasting shame is from the enemy.

> *For the sorrow that is according to the will of God produces a repentance without regret, leading to salvation, but the sorrow of the world produces death.*
>
> 2 Corinthians 7:10

Religion sets standards for holiness that are unattainable on our own. Ironically, religion also separates us from the power of God that enables us to walk in holiness. It's a double-edged sword that swings both ways.

❖ How does a son view holiness?

A son wants to be holy. He does not want anything to hinder intimate relationship with the Father. As a son, I am not separated *from* things. My holiness is based on who I am separated *unto*... and that is the Father.

Sons don't want anything to hinder their relationship with the Lord. It is the most important thing in their lives. Why? Because he is our source. He is our Father. We are vested already in the estate, and so, everything we need is supplied in due time, as the Father sees that we are ready.

CONDITION

❖ How does a child see his condition?

A child, if he's honest with himself, sees his condition as one of bondage and helplessness. He knows the things he can't escape from. He gets over one thing and something else happens. He's able to climb out of a pit but gets pulled back into a deeper pit. He calls it bad luck, poor choices, wrong place at the wrong time, but deep inside, he knows the fault lies with him. He just can't face it. He can't catch a break, and he doesn't know why. That is bondage. That is a child mentality.

Child to Son

- ❖ **How does a son see his condition?**

A son sees liberty as the overarching condition of this life, even when things are running contrary to his desired direction.

> *Consider it all joy, my brothers and sisters, when you encounter various trials, knowing that the testing of your faith produces endurance. And let endurance have its perfect result, so that you may be perfect and complete, lacking in nothing.*
>
> James 1:2-4

> *Blessed is a man who perseveres under trial; for once he has been approved, he will receive the crown of life which* the Lord *has promised to those who love Him.*
>
> James 1:12

When we're going through difficulties, we are to persevere. Embrace joy as we endure all kinds of temptations or trials in our lives. It is not a sign of failure; it is a sign of threat. We are a threat to the devil. When we endure difficulties; when we press through them; then we will receive the crown of life. Hallelujah!

Don't know if you can bear it? Yes, you can. Keep reading:

> *You are from God, little children, and have overcome them; because greater is He who is in you than he who is in the world.*
>
> 1 John 4:4

We have liberty. We are free. Yeah, I know all hell's breaking loose. Doesn't matter. I am still free. These things that are going on around me, I have a choice as a son to let them affect me or not. Does that mean I don't deal with them? No. It means the way that I deal with them is different from the way a child deals with them.

A child will say: "It is bondage. I can't take anymore. I'm stuck."

A son will say: "I'm free. This thing has no power in my life to bind me or to dictate where I am going or what I am doing. I am overcoming this thing by the blood of the Lamb and the word of my testimony."

The perspective we choose determines whether we are operating as a child or a son.

EXPRESSION OF LOVE

❖ **How does a child approach love?**

A child is guarded; his love is conditional. It is based on others' performance as he seeks to get his own needs met. That's why a lot of marriages break up. Two people have child mentalities, consequently, their love is conditional and guarded.

Surely, he doesn't love me, because he won't let me do this.

Surely, she doesn't love me if she won't do that.

❖ **How does a son approach love?**

A son is open, patient and affectionate. We lay down our life and our agendas to meet the needs of other people. We take the guise of a servant. We are sons who serve. Jesus had a phenomenal approach to servanthood.

> *Have this attitude in yourselves which was also in Christ Jesus, who, as He already existed in the form of God, did not consider equality with God something to be grasped, but emptied Himself by taking the form of a bond-servant and being born in the likeness of men. And being found in appearance as a man, He humbled Himself by becoming obedient to the point of death: death on a cross.*
>
> Philippians 2:5-8

> *[Jesus] got up from supper and laid His outer garments aside; and He took a towel and tied it around Himself. Then He poured water into the basin, and began washing the disciples' feet and wiping them with the towel which He had tied around Himself.*
>
> John 13:4-5

He wore a towel on his arm; he bent down and washed the feet of his disciples. Could he have been any more humble?

A son lays down his life and agenda to meet the needs of other people. Jesus was about meeting other people's needs. It was an expression of his love.

GOD'S PRESENCE

- ❖ **How does a child sense the presence of God?**

To a child, the presence of God is conditional and distant. They think they need to do this or that to get God and his presence in their life. If they do enough things; if they sing loud enough; work hard enough; pray long enough; read their Bible enough, then God's presence will come into their life. In the end, they only manage to burn themselves out.

- ❖ **How does a son sense the presence of God?**

A son sees the presence of God as close and intimate. All we must do is ask for it. *Father, I have some time. I'd love to spend it with you.* Next thing we know, God shows up. We don't have to sing, shout, dance or contort our souls. We just have to ask and he's there. It almost seems as if he was always there and that it was our perception of his presence that changed. *Almost*...ya know?

SPIRITUAL AMBITION

- ❖ **How does a child approach desire and ambition?**

A child willingly strives for spiritual achievement and distinction, based on a desire to be seen and counted among the great ones. A child's ambition is focused on himself; God is merely the means to an end. Unfortunately, such ambition does not end well.

- ❖ **How does a son approach desire and ambition?**

Following Jesus' example, sons and daughters in the kingdom will be servants of all.

A son experiences daily the Father's unconditional love and acceptance and is sent as a representative of God's love for others. We are not driven and drawn. Our motivation is experiencing the Father's unconditional love. When all hell is breaking loose and everything that could go wrong is going wrong, sons are chill. They are calm, collect and assured. Why? Because they rest in God's unconditional love.

SECURITY

- ❖ **How does a child respond to security?**

A child is deeply insecure and lacks inner peace. It is not a condition from ignorance, however, but of knowledge. A child, in our context, is still a child of God. They are simply immature ones. As such, they have some awareness that comes from the ongoing work of Holy Spirit. They are being shown the truth, albeit an inconvenient truth.

Their struggle is in growing up—as in whether to do so or not. In this condition, they are at war with themselves and the guardians and tutors who the Father has sent. They are faced with a reality they cannot accept: that they are immature, and that the journey to maturity requires letting go of their childish ways. Their insecurity and lack of peace, therefore, is self-inflicted.

- ❖ **How does a son respond to security?**

Scripture says that sons have a peace that passes all understanding.

> *And the peace of God, which surpasses all comprehension, will guard your hearts and minds in Christ Jesus.*
>
> Philippians 4:7

Child to Son

Sons know how to rest and be at peace. Peace is different from joy; it is different from happiness. At the local taverns, they have *happy hour*. It's the offer of a chemically induced, emotional experience that often leads to headaches, DWIs, and astounding bar bills (despite the promised discount). Funny how you never see advertised a *peace hour*. Why? Because we can't get peace from an emotional experience.

Peace is first and foremost a place to abide. It is where we are established, rooted and grounded. People look at us and wonder: *Why is she not out of her mind. Why is he not jumping off a bridge? Why are they not divorced? Why is she not running around crazy, thinking about her lunatic children?*

It is because we have a peace, and peace sustains us. It is the security that sons and daughters carry throughout their lives.

THEOLOGY

- ❖ **What is the theology of a child?**

A child lives by the love of the law. We find spiritual children in churches, beating people over the heads with the five-pound Bibles that their grandmother bought from a traveling salesman who was out on parole and needed a steady job. They like to convict us. *You did this, so this is going to happen in your life. You have to keep the law, keep the law, keep the law, keep the law! When in doubt, thou shalt not. You have to do everything right because if you don't, you are going straight to hell.* And they should know; that's where they got their message from!

- ❖ **What is the theology of a son?**

Sons live by the law of love. God's love for us is so pervasive, it permeates all that we are and do.

> *For in Him we live and move and exist, as even some of your own poets have said, "For we also are His descendants."*
>
> Acts 17:28

As sons, we are to love people with the same love that God loves us with. We are an expression of God's love: forgiving, gracious, liberating, even challenging.

> We open the doors to the church as we open our hearts to all people. We don't make anyone sit on the back row—real or metaphorically.

Now, there is this idea that we are supposed to agree with everybody. Not so. When we love someone, it doesn't mean we accept everything about them. It means we look past the sin, the aberrant lifestyle, the poor choices, and the struggles. If we didn't, we'd never reach anybody with the love of God. (And if God didn't look beyond our faults, his love would never have reached us.)

There have been homosexual couples in the churches I have led. We were glad to have them. We did not meet them at the door and withstand them because "you are living in sin." As a matter of fact, this was the very place they needed to be—in the church, hearing a doctrine of love they have never heard before. It's not a matter of getting right and then coming to church. If that was the case, there'd be a lot of empty pews and a few empty pulpits. Because if we find the perfect church, we are going to mess it up when we walk in. (Don't ask me how I know.)

Of course, extending the heart-felt love of God to another person does not mean we agree, accept and affirm their lifestyle. As a matter of fact, they didn't ask us, now did they? They probably came looking for some love, a bit of acceptance, and.... oh, I don't know. Hope!

We love sinners. We don't want to see them go to hell. We don't want to see them miss their purpose and destiny in life. We want to see them become who God created them to be. We do not approve of iniquity, nor do we single out a particular iniquity...especially the ones that make us cringe.

Mostly, the church is OK with gluttony. *Need an extra-wide pew? No problem. We'll have the crane set you down right over here.*

Child to Son

Just got divorced and remarried for the fourth time? *Hey, as long as you married a Christian.*

So that's your phone? *Mind if we check the text messages to your secretary?*

The key is this: We open the doors to the church as we open our hearts to all people. We don't make anyone sit on the back row—real or metaphorically. If they want to sit on the front, we'll make room. *Here's a free set of ear plugs.*

We draw the line at leadership, however. *You're not going to take the offering. You're not going to work in the nursery. You are in a state of recovery. You need the Word of God and the love from God's people. You've come to the right place. We'll help you, but sin is sin. This is why we are here.*

Our theology is not the love of the law, but the law of love. Sometimes, love is tough, but it's also easy when God's doing the convicting. For only he knows the right time to bring someone to repentance. The law confronts. Love converts.

As God's sons and daughters, let us walk in the law of love.

8

Conclusion

IN A NORMAL SEQUENCE OF EVENTS, a born-again believer starts their spiritual life as a child: immature, naive, yet hungry for more of God. He or she progresses to sonship, being led by the same Holy Spirit who brought him or her to salvation. The traits and inexperience that mark them as a child are being reworked. The unregenerated areas of the believer's being—that which the Bible calls "flesh"—are gradually being reclaimed as they submit and surrender to the ongoing sanctifying work of Holy Spirit. In a word: *growth*.

What happens, however, when the spiritual child doesn't grow? Such is the case when Christians don't realize that growth is even a thing. Sure, they've been born again, most likely they've emerged from some dark lifestyle and gnarly conditions. They are presently in love with Jesus and the sense of cleanliness invading their being. This much is good, but unless and until they embrace the process of sonship, their immaturity will calcify, and a child mentality will become the new normal.

They'll assume that they've arrived, that they're walking in the fullness of the Spirit, that being "a fool for Jesus" means walking by faith. They'll take every day as a new experience because they haven't the capacity to plan any further.

This situation is compounded when those surrounding the newly minted born-again believer are in the same condition. The child looks around, sees comfort in company, and blissfully flows with the prevailing scene. They embrace the psalmist's refrain (Marley, not David): "Don't worry about a thing... 'Cause every little thing, gonna be alright."

And it *is* alright...until it's time to grow up, take some responsibility and accept accountability. It's often said of this stage that "reality sets in." I don't like that phrase. Reality is what you make it. But what people mean is that the bills come due, the wolf's at the door, and the mailman no longer delivers. The pseudo-reality of living in a world rife with sin has been kept at bay for a season while the new believer finds his legs. He now approaches adolescence—that wonderful time of shock and "awe crap!" It's when childhood and adulthood eclipse each other in the murky waters of a dark harbor, and the child-bride senses a clarion call to something more...but what? Childhood has a purpose—to gather strength to grow into sons and daughters. Childhood is not a destination; it is a launch. But not everyone knows this.

Being an emergent son or daughter means realizing that everything we believed as a new convert might not necessarily be true. Prayers don't get answered as readily as they once did. People we thought were pure turn out to be human after all. Trust that once was returned to us with interest now feels like a gash in the landscape of our nascent vulnerability. It's the spiritual equivalent of skinned knees and diaper rash.

Unless we understand what is happening, we could easily lose our faith. Thankfully, the conversion experience—that moment in space and time where the Holy Spirit overshadows us and a holy seed is deposited—is hard to discredit. Much of what comes after that, however, is a different story. Lying church members, mediocre sermons, terrible sound systems and shrieking sopranos who think God is deaf—yes, we can probably do without those. But what sustains us through our metamorphosis is the presence of God himself

Conclusion

forming within us. Nothing around us is perfect in human form. Our help comes from the Lord, maker of heaven and earth.

When all else fails, God is trustworthy. In his love, he sends teachers who patiently (mostly) instruct us in the way we should go. We learn about sonship. We appreciate the difference between being a child, an orphan or a servant compared to being a mature son or daughter. We see what it is to grow, and we gather courage for the journey; for the joy set before us, we endure the cross. Without a vision, the people fail.

This book represents a vision of growth, of maturity, of the journey to becoming sons and daughters of God's kingdom. It's important that you embrace the process. If you don't like where you are—and most people don't—take courage, for it is bound to get worse. You are part of a process, something bigger than your present self. You are growing into that which has yet to fully appear. You are being perfected. You have the promise: "*But* when the perfect comes, the partial will be done away with" (1 Corinthians 13:10).

Take heart! Be strong. Be unflinchingly real, both with others and with yourself. There is more to this life than meets the eye. In a very real sense, only the strong survive; the weak do not. For too long, we have embraced the teaching that God's strength is made perfect in our weakness, *so be weak*. That's a perversion of what scripture says. The purpose of encountering our weakness is to supplant it with strength—the strength that flows from the heart of relationship with our Father. Said another way: we can be weak because he is strong, but weakness by itself accomplishes nothing. Ours is a union with our Father. We are growing, maturing, and it is he who is cultivating us.

Maturity, therefore, has a purpose. It is not to get the front row at conventions. It's not for a padded seat with our name on it, or a full calendar of speaking engagements. It's not for the adoring looks from young believers. It is not for the glimmer of eternal spring. It is to be made fit for service. Think of it: would a king go to war with an army of immature believers or an army of seasoned warriors?

Sonship According to the Kingdom

The call is to us, and to others. We who are of age, let us offer a hand up to those navigating the slippery rocks of God's holy mountain. Nothing says "growth" like helping others grow. The teacher offers, and the student receives.

I offer this teaching as one of many. It's not perfect, but I have made it as perfect as it needs to be to usher you into the arms of the loving Father; to his arms that console, comfort, and yet draw you into the power of your true identity: sonship.

So be like lights
On the rim of the water
Giving hope in a storm sea of night
Be a refuge amidst the slaughter
For these fugitives in their flight
For you are timeless and part of a puzzle
You are winsome and young as a lad
And there is no disease or no struggle
That can pull you from God
Be ye glad.

Be Ye Glad by Michael K Blanchard
© New Spring Publishing, Inc.

Appendix

Sources for this book are found here.

SHEPHERD THOUGHTS

Adoption differs from what we call adoption today. It describes how a Roman parent would formally and legally acknowledge his son's promotion from child to adult. This promotion would end the intrusive micromanagement of guardians and entrust the child with adult-level responsibility, decision-making freedom, and access to the family estate.

This kind of adoption could involve two kinds of people.

- A man's actual, biological children. They would be "adopted" as adult sons when the father determined they were ready.
- Someone outside the immediate or biological family, like our adoptions today. This would occur when a father acknowledged a faithful slave, the son of a friend, or some other person as an adult participant in his estate.

Perhaps the most famous Roman adoption is when Julius Caesar adopted Augustus Caesar. Augustus was a great-nephew to Julius and since Julius had no heir to the position of Caesar and no inheritor for his will, he adopted Julius as his son at eighteen years of age. This practice occurred other times as well, when a Roman emperor approached the end of his life with no heir, he would adopt an adult man whom he believed would rule well in his place.

This arrangement helps us understand what Paul is saying here. Both Jews (biological descendants of Abraham) and non-Jews (outside observers) received the blessing of a right relationship with God through faith in Christ, not through obeying the law. We're not just "added to God's family" so to speak, but we're recognized as responsible, trustworthy adults whom God desires to manage his resources and carry out his will on his behalf.

https://shepherdthoughts.com/baptistchurchny/adopted-as-sons-and-heirs/

CHRISTIANITY IN VIEW

The word adoption in the New Testament is translated from the Greek word *huiothesia*, which means "the placing of an adult son" and refers to the formal act of recognizing the maturity of an adult son. The word is found in five New Testament passages: Rom. 8:15,23: 9:4; Gal. 4:5; Eph. 1:5.

To the people living in the predominantly Greek and Roman culture of the 1st Century A.D., the word *huiothesia* would bring to mind the ceremony of *toga virilis*, in which a 14-year-old boy went through an investiture ceremony with the adult male members of his family, likely the father. At this ceremony, speeches of challenge to the youth would be made, and offerings would be made to the gods. Then, the boy would stand in the center of the group and take off the child's garment that he wore. A new adult man's robe, or *toga*, would be placed on him. This was the *toga virilis*, the "robe of a man".

http://christianityinview.com/biblestudies/adoption.html

GERALD COWEN

The Greek word: *Huiothesia* (adoption) is formed by combining *huios* (son) and *thesis* (a placing) and literally means "the placing as a son" or "adoption."

In the Greek world the word is found only as early as the second century B.C.; however, the concept of adoption (place a son) is much earlier. In Crete (fifth century B.C.) adoption had "to take place on the market-square before the assembled citizens and from the speaker's tribunal."

Appendix

https://www.sermonindex.net/modules/articles/index.php?view=article&aid=33490 ©2002-2023 SermonIndex.net Promoting Genuine Biblical Revival

While adoption is not the way we get into God's family, it is the way we come to fully enjoy God's family. "Adoption gives us the rights of sons. Regeneration gives us the nature of children: we are partakers of both of these, for we are sons." (Spurgeon) In other words, we get into God's family by regeneration (being "born again" = the new birth) when we are "born of the Spirit" (Jn 3:7-9), for "as many as received Him, to them He gave the right to become children (literally "born ones") of God, even to those who believe in His name." (Jn 1:12) In regeneration the Spirit makes us children of God, while in adoption He gives us the position, privilege and responsibilities of the "sons of God." God could have regenerated us (a new life), but, praise His Holy Name, He also graced us with adoption as His sons.

As Wayne Grudem says, "When we begin to realize the excellence of these blessings (as adopted sons of God), and when we appreciate that God has no obligation to give us any of them, then we will be able to exclaim with the apostle John, 'How great is the love the Father has lavished (bestowed profusely) on us, that we should be called children of God. And that is what we are!'" (1 Jn 3:1 NIV) Indeed, "How Great Thou Art!"

https://www.preceptaustin.org/adoption

CHARLES SPURGEON

They are children of His family, and come to Him as children come to a father, with loving confidence. Think of being made a son of God, a son of Him that made the heavens, a son of Him who is God over all, blessed forever. Can any man deserve that? Certainly not. This also must come as a gift.

(Perfect Praise, Charles Haddon Spurgeon)

P. H. DAVIDS

Adoption, however, is not entirely a past event. The legal declaration may have been made and the Spirit may have been given as a down payment, but the consummation of the adoption awaits the future, for adoption includes "the redemption of our bodies" (Ro 8:23). Thus adoption is something hoped for (cf 1 Jn 3:2, 3) as well as something already possessed. Adoption, then, is deliverance from the past (cf regeneration and justification), our position and our way of life in the present (walking by the Spirit, sanctification), and our future blessed hope (redemption of our bodies at the resurrection, glorification). It describes the process of becoming a son of God (cf. John 1:12; 1 John 3:1–2) and receiving an inheritance from God (cf. Col. 3:24).

(Daniel J. Treier and Walter A. Elwell, *Evangelical Dictionary of Theology*, Baker Academic, 1984, 2001, 2017)

WARREN W. WIERSBE

We are now heirs and joint heirs with Christ. That means everything we inherit comes through Christ. There are two names on the check: Our Lord Jesus signs the check, and we have to sign the check. This is what prayer is all about. This is why we come "in the name of Jesus," because apart from Him we can inherit nothing. You and I were born rich in Jesus Christ. We have the riches of His grace, the riches of His wisdom, and the riches of His mercy. We can draw upon all of His riches in glory by Christ Jesus....

Are you living up to (or squandering) your privileges? If you are a Christian, you have been adopted, you have an adult standing in the family of God. With this standing comes responsibility. We don't run away from suffering. We don't waste our inheritance. We are sure that we are born again, and we share this with others. We have the privilege of speaking to and for God and the freedom of walking with God. What privileges we have!

Appendix

(Wiersbe, Warren, *Key Words of the Christian Life—Understanding and Applying Their Meanings*, Baker Books, 2002)

A. H. Leitch

Adoption is the embracing and restoration of the prodigal son. It is not so much the analogy of the judge setting the prisoner free as it is a father restoring his son—the robe, the ring, the feast, the celebration (cf. Lk. 15:22–32). The emphasis in adoption is always an ethical one, and although it has been initiated and is constantly sustained through God's grace, it focuses constantly on response in the conscious experience of the believer.

(J. D. Douglas, Silva, M., & Tenney, M. C. *The Zondervan Encyclopedia of the Bible*, Zondervan, 1987, 2011)

Jerry Bridges

Consider that every sin you commit is an act of rebellion against the sovereign authority of God, or, as someone has said, an act of cosmic treason. So here we sit on death row, condemned as rebels, awaiting our execution. But instead of the death we deserve, we are made sons and daughters of the very King we have rebelled against. Instead of death, we get eternal life. Instead of wrath, we receive favor. Instead of eternal ruin, we are made heirs of God and coheirs with Christ. All this happened without our doing a single thing to earn the King's favor, or any attempt on our part to make restitution for our rebellion. His Son has done it all for us.

(Jerry Bridges, *The Gospel for Real Life*, NavPress, 2003)

Merrill Unger

Regeneration (means) the reproduction of the filial character, and adoption the restoration of the filial privilege. Adoption is a word of position rather than relationship. Adoption is not a putting into the family by spiritual birth, but a putting into the position of sons. The believer's relation to God as a child results from the new birth (John 1:12–13), whereas adoption is the divine act whereby one who is already a child is, through redemption from the law, placed in the position of an adult son (Gal. 4:1–5).

https://www.preceptaustin.org/adoption

J. I. PACKER

Paul teaches that the gift of justification (i.e., present acceptance by God as the world's Judge) brings with it the status of sonship by adoption (i.e., permanent intimacy with God as one's heavenly Father, Gal. 3:26; 4:4-7). In Paul's world, adoption was ordinarily of young adult males of good character to become heirs and maintain the family name and riches. Paul, however, proclaims God's gracious adoption of persons of bad character to become "heirs of God and co-heirs with Christ" (Rom. 8:17).

Justification is the basic blessing, on which adoption is founded; adoption is the crowning blessing, to which justification clears the way.

(J. I. Packer, *Concise Theology: A Guide to Historic Christian Beliefs; God Makes His People His Children*, Tyndale House Publishers, Inc., 1993)

W. E. VINE

In Eph. 1:5 they are said to have been foreordained unto "adoption as sons" through Jesus Christ, RV; the KJV, "adoption of children" is a mistranslation and misleading. God does not "adopt" believers as children; they are begotten as such by His Holy Spirit through faith. "Adoption" is a term involving the dignity of the relationship of believers as sons; it is not a putting into the family by spiritual birth, but a putting into the position of sons.

(W. E. Vine, *Vine's Expository Dictionary of New Testament Words*, Thomas Nelson, 1996)

Appendix

LEWIS SPERRY CHAFER

The New Testament Meaning.

The spiritual use of the word *adoption* signifies the placing of a child—in point of maturity—into the position of privilege and responsibility attached to an adult son. Here an important distinction appears between two Greek words, namely, *teknion*—used to denote little children who are under the authority of parents, tutors, and governors (cf. John 13:33)—and *huios*—used to denote an adult son....

In its distinctive significance, spiritual adoption means that the one thus placed has at once all the privilege—which is that of independence from tutors and governors—and liberty of a full-grown man. The Christian is enjoined to "stand fast" in the liberty wherewith Christ has made him free and not to be "entangled again with the yoke of bondage," which is evidently a reference to the legal or merit system (Gal. 5:1). Spiritual adoption also imposes the responsibilities belonging to full maturity....

Adoption assumes a practical meaning as set forth in the Galatian and Roman Epistles. In the former it becomes a deliverance from slavery, from guardians, and from nonage; in the latter it signifies a deliverance from the flesh (cf. Rom. 8:14–17). All of this is directly due to the new, complete responsibility which full maturity imposes and to the divine plan that the believer's life is to be lived from the start in the power of the Holy Spirit.

(Lewis Sperry Chafer, *Systematic Theology*, Kregel, 1993)

WARREN WIERSBE

Adoption describes a special relationship with the Father called "adoption," which must not be confused with adoption in the Western world. In the New Testament, adoption is the act of God whereby He gives each of His children an adult standing in the family. You do not get into God's family by adoption but by regeneration. Why? Because an adopted child does not have the same nature as his adoptive parents. God's children have God's own nature because they have been born of God's Spirit (2 Pet. 1:4). Adoption has to do with our standing in the family. It simply means that God treats us as adults, not as babes, and gives us adult privileges. For example, a baby does not even know he is a baby, and he certainly does not know his own parents. Even if a baby did know his own father, he would not be able to speak to him. But God's children know they are God's children! They not only know who their Father is, but they are able to speak to him and call him "Abba [Papa], Father!" For the most part, children live in bondage and fear until they are old enough to care for themselves; but God's children are free from both bondage and fear. Why does God adopt his children and give them an adult standing in the family? So that they will have the freedom to draw upon all his resources and grow into mature sons and daughters. We are free to walk with him and talk with him, free to hear his Word and follow his Spirit. Even though we constantly need to grow, we do so in a family atmosphere of freedom and grace, not bondage and law.

(Warren W. Wiersbe, *Be What You Are*, Tyndale House Pub, 1988)

WAYNE DETZLER

Adoption in the Greek and Roman world was a beautiful picture. His contemporary culture gave the Apostle Paul this word, but he gave the word a new, Holy Spirit-inspired meaning. No concept is more meaningful to a believer....

Throughout the Greek world the wealthy and influential practiced adoption. Sometimes just a simple declaration in the marketplace turned a child into a son.

For adoption deposits everything that God owns to the accounts of His sons and daughters. Adoption is all about position and privilege...

(Wayne E. Detzler, *New Testament Words in Today's Language*. Victor, 1986)

Appendix

QUOTATIONS

Here are some quotes I've collected over the years as I taught on sonship. Alas, the specific locations have been lost, but the wisdom remains timeless.

******

The word adoption has to do with placing one in a position of privilege and responsibility.

Dwight Pentecost

That we who have forfeited and lost our place and privileges as children of God may be fully reinstated therein was one of the great teachings of Jesus Christ. For that the parable of the prodigal son was spoken.

Merrill Unger

Writing to a new generation after World War II, Winston Churchill challenged:

You have not an hour to lose.... Don't be content with things as they are. 'The earth is yours and the fullness thereof.' Enter your inheritance; accept your responsibility.

Oh, that believers would enter their inheritance and accept their responsibility as sons and daughters of God!

Winston Churchill

"Oh," said a worldling to me when I was in great pain and weakness of body, "is this the way God treats His children? Then I am glad I am not one."

How my heart burned within me, and my eyes flashed, as I said that I would take an eternity of such pain as I endured sooner than stand in the place of the man who preferred ease to God. I felt it would be hell to me to have a doubt of my adoption, and whatever pain I might suffer was a trifle so long as I knew that the Lord was my God.

Charles Spurgeon

Sonship According to the Kingdom

I would not change places with the wealthiest and most influential person in the world. I would rather be a child of the King, a joint-heir with Christ, a member of the Royal Family of heaven!

Billy Graham

Adoption

BEHOLD what wondrous grace
The Father hath bestow'd
On sinners of a mortal race,
To call them sons of God!

'Tis no surprising thing,
That we should be unknown:
The Jewish world knew not their King,
God's everlasting Son.

Nor doth it yet appear
How great we must be made;
But when we see our Saviour here,
We shall be like our Head.

A hope so much divine
May trials well endure,
May purge our souls from sense and sin,
As Christ the Lord is pure.

If in my Father's love
I share a filial part,
Send down Thy Spirit, like a dove,
To rest upon my heart.

We would no longer lie
Like slaves beneath the throne;
My faith shall Abba Father cry,
And Thou the kindred own.

by **Isaac Watts**, 1709

About the Author

GREG HOOD WAS BORN AND RAISED IN AMORY, MISSISSIPPI, and has been in ministry for over 37 years. He is the President and Founder of Greg Hood Ministries, The Network of Five-Fold Ministers and Churches, as well as Kingdom University. All are based in the United States of America. He is the lead apostle at Kingdom Life Ekklesia in Franklin, Tennessee.

Greg apostolically leads many leaders and churches around the globe. He and his wife, Joan, are planters of apostolic centers and have pioneered several apostolic centers within the United States and throughout the world. Greg and Joan travel extensively, empowering believers for the passionate pursuit of their God-given mandate, resulting in personal and societal transformation. Their greatest passion is to see the Body of Christ come to its fullness within the Kingdom of God. Greg is driven with great passion to speak into the lives of those who are called into leadership to the Church, Government, and the Marketplace. He burns to see people become who God has fashioned them to be.

Greg and Joan, have been married for 26 years. The Hood's base their ministry headquarters in Franklin, Tennessee.

Previous Work

The Gospel of the Kingdom.

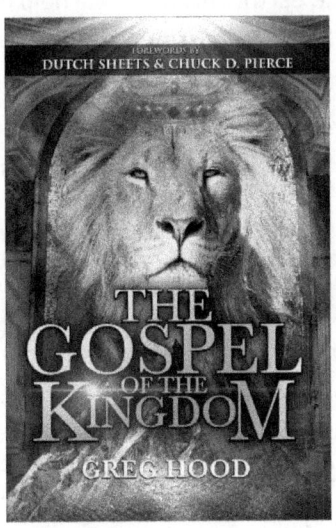

My friend, Greg Hood, is not only a teacher of the Word, but he is a student. Ever learning, ever maturing...as we all should be. The concepts and truth in this book may be new to you and that's okay. They are based on Scripture yet are just coming into their season. Kingdom, Kingdom Connection, Ekklesia, Apostles, Reigning in Life and so much more within these pages that will inspire you and encourage you and above all, change you. I encourage you to grab a cup of coffee, open your hearts and minds to what God is saying and doing, and take notes! Get ready to grow.

Tim Sheets, Apostle
Author of *Angel Armies, Angel Armies on Assignment, Planting the Heavens*
Tim Sheets Ministries
The Oasis Church, Middletown, Ohio

In *The Gospel of the Kingdom,* my friend Greg Hood gives us language that stirs our hearts with a fresh passion to see God's governmental rule manifested in the earth. This book will help develop in you a heart for that which God Himself is passionate about. Let it stir you with that which stirs Him, the redemption of all things back to Himself.

Robert Henderson
Best-Selling Author, *Courts of Heaven Series*

The Gospel of the Kingdom will revolutionize how believers live out the mission and mandate of Christ to change our world. Apostle Greg Hood brings a fresh approach to this vital topic which will empower members of Christ's Ekklesia to use their God given authority to cause God's Kingdom to come & will to be done on earth as it is in heaven.

Jane Hamon, Apostle
Vision Church

Apostolic and Prophetic voices everywhere agree that the church, the ekklesia, has shifted into a new age, a new Reformation. In his book, *The Gospel of the Kingdom*, Dr. Greg Hood challenges believers to shift out of a mindset of practicing a religion into one of fulfilling God's original Kingdom mandate to redeem and restore the earth. As God's earthly ambassadors of His Kingdom, we must grasp the authority and responsibility invested in us, and to examine scripture in a fresh light and understanding so that we can cause the kingdoms of this world to become the kingdoms of our Lord and of his Christ.

Tom Hamon, Apostle
Vision Church

Previous Work

Dr. Greg Hood has written a very necessary book for the body of Christ at this critical time. It is an apostolic foundation for us to stand upon and will give context and order to our Kingdom call. *The Gospel of the Kingdom* has been written by a scholar who loves the word of God and has communicated in a fresh and direct way exactly what the Lord was sent by the Father to do and why we are being equipped, "For such a time as this". The Kingdom assignments that are before us will require binding the strongman and plundering the enemy.

Anne S. Tate
International Director of Prayer and the Watches
Glory of Zion, International

The Gospel of the Kingdom is one of the most important messages that undergirds much of our understanding of Scripture and the relationship between man and God. Jesus who was a perfect man and God incarnate made the Gospel of the Kingdom the essence of his preaching while he was on earth making the Gospel of the Kingdom the most important message Jesus ever preached and that he expects his followers all over the world to emulate. I am convinced that much of the body of Christ is weak because of a lack of understanding of the Gospel of the Kingdom. My dear friend Dr. Greg Hood's book completely changes that unfortunate trajectory by reintroducing much of the body of Christ to the Gospel of the Kingdom. I highly recommend this powerful book for anyone who is serious about personal transformation and the transformation of culture.

Dr. Francis Myles
Author: *The Order of Melchizedek*
Founder: Francis Myles International

THIS BOOK! Here it is, an astoundingly simple yet profound picture of the Kingdom of God. Greg does such a great job of bringing the truth out about God's original intention, what He had in mind to do, from "...before the foundation of the world." This book clears up all the questionable things we have heard and been taught regarding His will, His character, His heart for humanity and His Kingdom purpose. It's a MUST-READ!

> **Apostle Randy Lopshire**
> Riverside Church
> Clarksville, TN

My family and I have gotten to know Greg and Joan Hood, not only in a spiritual leadership way, but also in a personal way.

They are true, kind and wise ... beyond their years

This book is an amazing read. Greg's wisdom and interpretation of scripture is so insightful and energizing! Everyone needs a copy of this book as a guideline for life and salvation! We are proud to know and love this man of God and have the utmost confidence in him.

> Shalom to all!
> **Lily Isaacs and the Isaacs Family**
> Members of the Grand Ole Opry

Rebuilding the Broken Altar – Awakening Out of Chaos.

This book is as loaded with keen insight and Spirit-inspired revelation as any we will find. We would be hard pressed to find a book more timely and more relevant for the Church and the nations—especially America—than Rebuilding the Broken Altar. Sadly, many books simply restate others' teachings, simply coloring them with a different spin. However, it is refreshing when I read a book that feeds me new thoughts and information. Simply stated, I was more than entertained and inspired by Greg's book—I learned a lot!

Dr. Dutch Sheets, Dutch Sheets Ministries and Give Him 15 daily prayer and decrees.
Bestselling author of: *Authority in Prayer, An Appeal to Heaven, Intercessory Prayer*

If there was ever a time when a people needed to return to the Lord it is now. In his book "Rebuilding the Broken Altar" Greg Hood gives insight to the necessary process of recovering ourselves from the snare of the devil and experiencing the blessing of God again as a people. I would encourage, as we read to allow the Holy Spirit to stir our hearts again with His passion for us individually and as a nation.

Robert Henderson
Best Selling Author of *The Courts of Heaven Series*

In *Rebuilding the Broken Altar*, Greg Hood presents a masterpiece of hope for the future of the church, for America and for nations crying out for a move of God. He carefully, Biblically and prophetically lays out a blueprint for revival that every leader and believer alike can work with to shift culture and engage the spiritual atmosphere to bring change. The word studies bring incredible insight and reveal the important elements necessary for rebuilding the altar of the Lord which has been broken down in both the church and in society in order to see an unprecedented outpouring from heaven, for harvest and transformation.

Dr. Jane Hamon, Vision Church @ Christian International
Author of: *Dreams and Visions, The Deborah Company, The Cyrus Decree, Discernment*

My friend Greg Hood is known as hard-hitting, straight-shooting and uncompromising in his preaching. His writing is even more so! I love the way he boldly challenges us to break free from old religious mindsets so that we can embrace God's kingdom plans. In his new book *Rebuilding the Broken Altar*, Greg gives us a clear vision of a restored church. With rich insights about the twelve tribes of Israel, he takes us on a journey toward the restoration of New Testament faith. We will be challenged and inspired!

J. Lee Grady, Author and Director of The Mordecai Project

Dr. Greg Hood helps us to understand the meaning of the time and grasp the seismic impact of the altar. I have had the privilege of Greg's friendship and the blessings of his clear prophetic voices. I praise the Lord Jesus for enabling him to write this valuable book.

Tamrat Layne, Former Prime Minister, Ethiopia

The bottom-line message of this book, God is not finished with we or America, but the church and some pastors and some of us in government need to get our stones together.

Rep. Gene Ward, PhD, Hawai'i House of Representatives

Kingdom University

KINGDOM UNIVERSITY offers accredited and degreed classes in:

- Christian Counseling
- Kingdom Studies
- Business
- Five-Fold Ministry
- Government Studies
- The Arts

CAMPUSES IN:

- Georgia
- Indiana
- Louisiana
- Missouri
- North Carolina
- Texas
- Illinois
- Kentucky
- Mississippi
- New Jersey
- Tennessee
- Online Campus

More campuses coming to a state near you!

INSTRUCTORS INCLUDE:

Dr. Greg Hood	Dr. Ron Phillips	Apostle Tommy Kelly
Dr. Dutch Sheets	Dr. Tod Zeiger	Apostle Bob Long
Dr. Tim Sheets	Dr. Tom Schlueter	Apostle Jacquie Tyre
Dr. Jane Hamon	Dr. Alemu Beeftu	Apostle Regina Shank
Dr. Tom Hamon	Dr. Scott Reece	Apostle Kerry Kirkwood
Dr. Dwain Miller		

Kingdom University meets one weekend a month on a Friday evening and a Saturday. School year is from January-November.

Register today by going to: www.KingdomU.org
Contact us at: Office@KingdomU.org
WE WILL SEE WE IN THE CLASSROOM!

www.ingramcontent.com/pod-product-compliance
Lightning Source LLC
Chambersburg PA
CBHW060511100426
42743CB00009B/1283